Question Power

Question Power

How They Can Change and Influence Instructional Practices

William Truesdale
Vinni M. Hall

ROWMAN & LITTLEFIELD
Lanham • Boulder • New York • London

Published by Rowman & Littlefield
An imprint of The Rowman & Littlefield Publishing Group, Inc.
4501 Forbes Boulevard, Suite 200, Lanham, Maryland 20706
www.rowman.com

86-90 Paul Street, London EC2A 4NE, United Kingdom

Copyright © 2025 by William Truesdale and Vinni M. Hall

All rights reserved. No part of this book may be reproduced in any form or by any electronic or mechanical means, including information storage and retrieval systems, without written permission from the publisher, except by a reviewer who may quote passages in a review.

British Library Cataloguing in Publication Information Available

Library of Congress Cataloging-in-Publication Data

Names: Truesdale, William, 1963– author. | Hall, Vinni M., 1942– author.
Title: Question power : how they can change and influence instructional practices / William Truesdale, Vinni M. Hall.
Description: Lanham, Maryland : Rowman & Littlefield, 2025. | Includes bibliographical references and index. | Summary: "Question Power: How They Can Change and Influence Instructional Practices outcome is to elevate instructional efficacy that rebuilds, renews, and regenerates learning through the power of questioning"— Provided by publisher.
Identifiers: LCCN 2024025764 (print) | LCCN 2024025765 (ebook) | ISBN 9781475869781 (cloth) | ISBN 9781475869798 (paperback) | ISBN 9781475869804 (epub)
Subjects: LCSH: Questioning. | Instructional systems—Design.
Classification: LCC LB1027.44 .T78 2025 (print) | LCC LB1027.44 (ebook) | DDC 371.3—dc23/eng/20240718
LC record available at https://lccn.loc.gov/2024025764
LC ebook record available at https://lccn.loc.gov/2024025765

∞™ The paper used in this publication meets the minimum requirements of American National Standard for Information Sciences—Permanence of Paper for Printed Library Materials, ANSI/NISO Z39.48-1992.

If I had an hour to solve a problem and my life depended on the solution, I would spend the first fifty-five minutes determining the proper question to ask, for once I know the proper question, I could solve the problem in less than five minutes.
—Albert Einstein

The Power of Questions: Questions ARE the Answer.
—Tony Robbins

Contents

Preface ix

Reader's Note xvii

Introduction: The Cornerstone (Quoin) of This Book: What Learner Outcomes Are Expected? 1

1 Metacognition/Executive Functioning for Both Educator and Learner: Using Questions 7

2 Teaching the Art of Questioning for Both Educator and Learner 23

3 Technology as a Useful Tool to Answer and Explore Questions 33

4 Motivating Learning by Throwing a Party 39

5 New/Old Instructional Strategies to Use 47

6 Instructional Consumerism: What Is It? 55

Postscript: Researchers That Influence Educators for All Learner Characteristics 63

Index 67

About the Authors 73

Preface

Designing/suggesting foundations that build instructional efficacy and ask challenging questions that keep both the educator and the learner engaged is presented in this small book. Using questions-asking strategies to motivate learners and educators to actively participate in understanding content and skills is offered to the reader.

Educators are in charge of the instructional architecture. Educators then "juggle" a myriad of variables to actually get to instruction and then make the learning "stick."[1] Some of these variables include: common core learning standards, scripted programs, professional development sessions, oceans of technology and digital programs, and the learners' foundational knowledge and experiences. This book is designed to suggest some ideas to create usable blueprints to guide learning episodes through questions that motivate discourse.

An architect planning and designing buildings must consider the aesthetic, sustainability, and functionality of any space. This book is written for educators who are instructional architects creating conversations and questions that open learning spaces. Opening up learning spaces leads to making sense of something; gaining consensus; generating ideas and possibilities; building relationships; looking for opportunities for self-influence; and making decisions. The ultimate goal for this book is to promote instructional efficacy using questions.

Instructional efficacy is the art of silence (giving time to process, think, and reflect), patience (offering wait time for connecting what is known with new knowledge), and asking questions that produce outcomes from learning episodes that are essential for active student (and educator/teacher) participation. Architects use the term *hierarchy* to help them build/design any project. Architects must consider foundational requirements, investments, and amass a team of talent—in other words, know what they are doing based on their own training and experience. Like the architect, educators have developed a hierarchy that allows interactive and reciprocal communication among the "investors" (learner, educator, parent, community, administrators). How can the tensions between what is on the test and what is in a life be mediated in the classroom using questioning strategies? Questioning with the expectation of cogent answers supports critical thinking, self-advocacy, and better decision-making.

BASIC QUESTIONS ADDRESSED IN THIS BOOK

Five questions are the foundation for designing instructional efficacy:

1. What possible instructional strategies, activities, and resources can educators use to teach students to learn how they learn and remember? (developing personal responsibility for learning)
2. How can an educator create an instructional blueprint for students to ask questions for continuous learning? (creating and motivating the learner to expand the life of the learning episode)
3. How can the educator help students to use technology effectively and efficiently for research; to check for authenticity; to sharpen skills; to promote task engagement; to practice; to memorize basic skills and concepts; and to connect and apply new knowledge to learned concepts and skills? (using tools that will ensure the application of rigor and relevance of the content and skills of any learning episode)
4. What general framework activities might educators use to reframe the passive learner to a more curious and active participant (especially after third grade)? (encouraging student voice and task participation in learning episodes)
5. What new/old strategies can be recycled, refreshed, and/or invented to build instructional efficacy? (tools for educators to achieve instructional efficacy)

How do we get students to ask questions like (1) "How did they do that?"; (2) "What is missing?"; (3) "What questions aren't answered in the information presented?"; (4) "What questions about who, what, when, where, or how did this get started?"; and (5) "What might be invented, done, created to be something better?"

WHAT POSSIBLE INSTRUCTIONAL STRATEGIES, ACTIVITIES, RESOURCES CAN EDUCATORS USE TO TEACH STUDENTS TO LEARN HOW THEY LEARN AND REMEMBER? (DEVELOPING PERSONAL RESPONSIBILITY FOR TEACHING AND LEARNING)

Metacognitive Teaching

What tools can educators add to their repertoires that may encourage executive functioning and intentionally develop metacognitive schemas for themselves? Metacognition is one's ability to think about one's thinking. It is about identifying one's own needs, monitoring mistakes, recognizing success and that includes self-reflection and self-regulation. It is about how one is effective by answering self-questions. A common set of executive functioning skills include the following:

1. Adaptable thinking—making decisions and choices to varying instructional practice
2. Planning/designing using journaling and listing to include essential concepts and skills
3. Self-monitoring for evaluating oneself, tracking steps that lead to goal completion
4. Self-control—thinking before acting and reacting (developing emotional intelligence)
5. Working memory (using short-term memory and step-by-step regimes (protocols) to "connect the dots" for themselves and their students
6. Time management—scheduling and prioritizing to meet goal setting and producing results
7. Organization—arranging thoughts, actions, and materials toward clarity, rhythm, and flow

Executive Functioning

Executive functioning supports (the learner and) educator to learn how they learn. Explicitly teaching students how to start a learning task can be done with a think aloud type of strategy. For example, if the educator wants students to write in a journal every day and/or respond to a writing prompt, use a "think out loud" or modeling protocol: What verbal cues did I hear about the task? Can I describe the task in my own words? If I don't understand, what or who can I ask or can I observe what others are doing? What materials do I need to complete the task? How is this task like other tasks that I have tried? The effective educator can deliberately use executive functioning as a planner themselves. In this chapter there is a chart that may aid in creating an executive functioning planner. The executive functioning is about thinking about how one thinks. The planner is to guide one on the path to learn about how they think.

Bandura[2] says a person can know about efficacy if they are engaged in the intrapersonal examination of their self-judgments. He offers four sources of self-efficacy: enactive experiences, verbal persuasion, vicarious experiences, and physiological arousal.

Some of the instructional strategies include speaking metacognitive language like "You might need some more folders to organize your math papers." "Where can you get some folders to help you organize your papers?" The greatest helping hand is at the end of your own arm. Activities that will be listed include examples such as developing a "mystery" board that lists suspects and clues. Why do I need to solve this mystery? What do I know? What do I want to know? What's missing? What are possible solutions?

HOW CAN AN EDUCATOR CREATE AN INSTRUCTIONAL BLUEPRINT FOR STUDENTS TO ASK QUESTIONS FOR CONTINUOUS LEARNING?
(CREATING AND MOTIVATING LEARNERS TO EXPAND THE LIFE OF THE LEARNING EPISODE)

Expanding the Life of a Learning Episode

Story: Have you ever watched a toddler: their first steps, words, sentences, and the delightful curiosity of making sense of their world? Mother or Father says: "Point to your ears, your eyes, your chin, your belly . . ." There is reciprocal joy. Then the toddler points to everything to develop the vocabulary. Parents point to an apple and anything round or red becomes an apple for our little toddler. Those initial requests like "Apple me" could be interpreted as "give me an apple" or "can I have an apple?" Fast forward to first days of schooling—those adoring eyes of a rapt audience (parents, guardians) are lost with this looming educator who must attend to many more faces, questions, and behaviors. How does an educator get that insatiable curiosity back in the lives of learners in the school setting? For the toddler, the adoring faces of the parents (guardians) excite their energy to learn along with the biological elasticity of the emerging brain function. How can school environs create algorithms, schemas, patterns that create the awe of learning?

How Does One Learn?

Educators have styles of teaching and philosophical leanings as to how students learn. Those philosophical leanings may influence the kinds of questions that are asked of students. Learning theories are a set of different concepts that explain, observe, describe the processes that one uses to acquire knowledge, skills, behaviors or develops competencies through practice, study, or experience. So we don't know, for sure, how one learns.

How does one learn something new? What does one do with the new learning? How does one learn to learn? There are many theories of learning. *All* learners and educators use a combination of these theories. These theories offer the reader a variety of ways to learn "playing cards": "know when to hold 'em, know when to fold 'em, know when to walk away" (Kenny Rogers song).[3] Learning theories in education usually fall into three broad categories: (1) Behaviorism (Skinner,[4] Pavlov[5])—Will this behaviorist leaning educator expect learners to "hurry up and wait" for expected response to stimuli presented?; (2) Cognitivism (Piaget,[6] Vygotsky[7])—Will this educator expect students to passively think about what has been presented with the results of assessment as clue as to what has been understood?; and/or (3) Constructivism (Dewey,[8] Bandura,[9] Freire[10])—Will this educator design plans for students to "get their hands dirty" by building and connecting their understanding of what has been taught to what they already know?

HOW CAN THE EDUCATOR HELP STUDENTS USE TECHNOLOGY EFFECTIVELY AND EFFICIENTLY?

How can the educator help students to use technology effectively and efficiently for research to check for authenticity; to sharpen skills; to promote task engagement; to practice; and to connect and apply new knowledge to learned concepts and skills?

Many of the world's students are "addicted" to too much screen time. Young teens are sitting across from one other on a "date" and each is on their respective phone. They are not interacting with each other. They miss visual social cues. One sees parents give young children a screen to calm or distract. Learning to turn off televisions, laptops, or smartphones is a formidable challenge. Instructional educators almost need to design distractions that allow students to look away; can't help but look; or find something so compelling that they are riveted by an image, a sound, a smell, or a touch in an authentic environment/reality. How do we instantiate supportive AI for education? What strategies can we use with technology to support student development in the following areas?

a. Truth, Trust, Safety
b. Research
c. Authenticity
d. Skill Sharpening
e. Task Engagement
f. Practice
g. Memory
h. Connecting and Applying New Knowledge to Learned Concepts and Skills
i. Managing AI (artificial intelligence)

WHAT GENERAL FRAMEWORK ACTIVITIES MIGHT EDUCATORS USE TO MOVE THE PASSIVE LEARNER TO BECOME A MORE CURIOUS AND ACTIVE LEARNER?

How does an educator awaken the social and emotional behaviors of passive learners to engage in learning about themselves and others? Learners are active when they are debating, discussing, demonstrating, experimenting, and practicing. Designing a blueprint of activities to support takes preparation time. Suggestions are offered to look for onboarding activities and parents, community, administrators, and so on to enhance active participation. How do you provide opportunities for students to have voice and choice in "innovative" activities? By taking polls among their fellow classmates on such things as favorite movies; asking the best way to solve word problems; and/or top three items to spend $100 on. Students can demonstrate by creating video commercials of their understanding around character and plot development in the story they are reading.

WHAT NEW/OLD STRATEGIES CAN BE RECYCLED, REFRESHED, AND/OR INVENTED TO BUILD INSTRUCTIONAL EFFICACY?

There is nothing new under the sun. Are there some tried and true instructional strategies that work with most learners to think about their own thinking, connect the old learnings to the new, and apply those learnings to make good decisions? Some researchers have enduring notions that continue to support teacher effectiveness.

* * *

The structure of the book includes the following six chapters:

Chapter 1: Metacognition/Executive Functioning for Both Educator and Learner: Using Questions
Chapter 2: Teaching the Art of Questioning for Both Educator and Learner
Chapter 3: Technology as a Useful Tool to Answer and Explore Questions
Chapter 4: Motivating Learning by Throwing a Party
Chapter 5: New/Old Instructional Strategies to Use
Chapter 6: Instructional Consumerism: What Is It?

NOTES

1. B. Goodwin, K. Rouleau, et al., *The New Classroom Instruction That Works: The Best Research-Based Strategies for Increasing Student Achievement* (McRel International and ASCD, 2022), https://www.mcrel.org/the-new-classroom-instruction-that-works-the-best-research-based-strategies-for-increasing-student-achievement-has-arrived/.
2. A. Bandura, "Self-Efficacy: Toward a Unifying Theory of Behavioral Change." *Psychological Review* 84, no. 2 (1977): 191–215, https://doi.org/10.1037/0033-295X.84.2.191.
3. Kenny Rogers, "The Gambler," 1978.
4. B. F. Skinner, *The Behavior of Organisms*, 1938.
5. I. Pavlov (1898), "Behaviorism in Psychology," 2024, https://www.psychology.org/behaviorism.html.
6. J. Piaget (1936), "Piaget's 4 Stages of Cognitive Development Explained," 2024, https://www.verywellmind.com/piagets-stages-of-cognitive-development-2795457.
7. L. Vygotsky (1962), "Vygotsky's Theory of Cognitive Development," 2024, www.simplypsychology.org/vygotsky.html.
8. J. Dewey (1859), "Constructivism Learning Theory & Philosophy of Education," 2024, www.simplypsychology.org/constructivism.html.
9. A. Bandura (1986), "From Neo-behaviorism to Social Constructivism: The Transformation of Albert Bandura's Research Paradigm." *Psychological Science (China)* 29, no. 1 (2006): 225–27, https://psycnet.apa.org/record/2006-04864-062.
10. Global Social Theory, Paulo Friere biography, 2024, https://globalsocialtheory.org/thinkers/freire-paulo/.

Reader's Note

The concept of teacher efficacy means mediating the tension among one's self (personal, internal, emotional), view of one's teaching influence, and one's perception of how external factors (parents, administration, and colleagues) influence teaching practices. This book's outcome is to elevate teachers to rebuild, renew, regenerate learning and instructional efficacy through the power of questioning. In the authors' opinion, educators have at times been described as "those who can't teach." There is not one aspect of anyone's life that has not been touched through a teacher/educator. Teacher/educator efficacy has been buffeted by education corporations selling ideas, writing scripts, and selling books. Teacher/educator efficacy has been influenced by the politics of banning books, banning words, and the fear of mass shootings. Teacher/educator efficacy has been challenged by parents, guardians, and administrations who do not value the strengths of the profession of teaching.

Introduction

The Cornerstone (Quoin) of This Book: What Learner Outcomes Are Expected?

The architectural definition of a quoin (pronounced "coin") or cornerstone of a building is the wedge-shaped stone demarking the placement of a structure on which the walls are placed. The quoin is where two walls intersect. The use of quoins or cornerstones dates to early Roman architecture and the emergence of stone-cutting techniques. During the Renaissance period, the quoin was a cost-effective technique to demonstrate the sought-after qualities of consistency and balance. The quoin of this book is about suggesting question-asking strategies to build structures and systems that promote lifelong learning habits.

Pedagogy (the art of educating) and architecture share many of the same set of skills. The educator and the architect must intentionally engage their respective audiences. Each does not build anything in a vacuum. They must balance a set of variables. Both architecture and pedagogy are influenced by and influence social, political, and psychological actions and reactions. Instructing today's learners requires designs that build content and skills using accepted standards to promote critical thinking about life's decisions. This hands-on book of ideas is designed to give educators strategies that motivate and develop student learning architectures that are functional and sustainable.

This book of ideas intentionally designs teaching episodes to get learners to fully participate in learning through the art of questioning. Educators are energized by the learners' reactions and engagement. What if an educator could enhance class participation by getting the learner to question and discuss more? This book is created to increase question-asking behaviors toward influencing educator pedagogy and student learning of content and skills needed after formal schooling in the pursuit of lifelong learning.

If a learner questions and discusses the content and skills, the more apt an educator/instructor will be to make room for mutual engagement. Questions ensure engagement, excitement, and active participation in the learning experience. The benefits of question-asking and answer exchanges allow for the understanding and/or diagnoses of comprehension of what is to be learned. Answers to educator questions by their students lead to the areas that need to be retaught. Prompting students to "ask" or "talk" increases language skills (i.e., vocabulary). Answers to learners' questions by an educator promote enrichment (more questions) and motivate learners to be actively involved in gaining competencies, increase language development, enhance critical thinking skills, and foster self-advocacy and self-reflection of their own learning strategies. This book will offer new strategies and review some old ones to create a question-asking blueprint for both educator and learner.

Teacher-designed questions tend to provide the quoin of teacher efficacy. Teacher efficacy and/or personal self-efficacy is the belief that suggests that one "can." Teachers/educators trust that they "can" personally influence, make responsible decisions, and reflect on the effectiveness of their pedagogy. Questions, dialogue, discussion, and communicative reciprocity support the cornerstone of what happens in classrooms.

> Teachers' beliefs in their efficacy affect their general orientation toward the education process as well as their specific instructional activities. Those who have a low sense of instructional efficacy favor a custodial orientation that takes a pessimistic view of students' motivation, emphasize control of classroom behavior through strict regulations, and rely on extrinsic inducements and negative sanctions to get students to study.... They distrust their ability to manage their classrooms; are stressed and angered by students' improvability ... focus more on subject matter than on students' development; and if they had to do it all over again, would not choose the teaching profession.[1]

REASONS FOR QUESTIONING THE PURPOSE OF EDUCATION

The authors were not around for the discoveries of fire and the wheel. However, the authors have served as classroom teachers, administrators, college professors, book reviewers, members of school boards and academic professional organizations. After evaluating and observing many educators in many settings (urban, suburban, and rural), it has become patently clear that after third grade learners' questions go from "Why is the sky blue?" to "How many pages do you want me to write?"; "When is the science project due?"; and the favorite: "Will this be on the test?"

What is the purpose of education? Is it to be a lifelong learner after formal schooling? How does an educator design at least some teaching episodes that motivate learners to be information processors, complex thinkers, effective communicators, willing collaborators, cooperators and self-reflectors, and self-regulators?

It seems now that the purpose of schooling is to do well on tests. Those standardized test results define a school as a good one or a struggling one. This testing is often tied to the evaluation of the educator (school administrators included), the learner, the public, and parental opinions. This testing is also tied to funding and school closings. Those standardized tests should not be the drivers of what schools should be about: "To live long and prosper." Those words uttered by Spock (half Vulcan) of the famed television series *Star Trek* are the launch pad for why this book is necessary.[2] Most of a learner's life is outside and after school. A learner's ability to learn how they learn is a necessary tool to live life and prosper.

> Standardized testing is at cross purposes with many of the most important purposes of public education. It doesn't measure big-picture learning, critical thinking, perseverance, problem solving, creativity or curiosity, yet those are the qualities great teaching brings out in a student.
> —Randi Weingarten (president of the American Federation of Teachers)[3]

Here are some of the dilemmas and challenges that educators report that must be considered, included, and managed as they teach and motivate their students/learners.

How Can Educators . . .

1. Facilitate teaching common core standards to students who have a poor grasp of foundational or background knowledge?
2. Teach students to make wise decisions as consumers?
3. Encourage students to watch or listen to the news and weather (road conditions, too) to know at least what clothes to wear?
4. Encourage students to participate in solving authentic issues (preparing a meal; developing a healthy diet; creating an exercise regime; participating in solving an ongoing community issue) toward social emotional well-being?

5. Create student inventors, discoverers, philosophers, scientists, and/or analysts to manage the future challenges and foster sustainability?
6. Change classrooms so that students are not passive recipients but active learners so school environments are more exciting?
7. Create curious lifelong learners?
8. Teach equity and collaboration?
9. Teach information processing?
10. Encourage students to participate and be part of a community?
11. Teach the difference between cooperation and competition? And balance the two?
12. Teach students to express themselves respectfully?
13. Teach students to protect the planet?
14. Teach social justice?
15. Manage, mentor, support, and coach students toward independence and self-advocacy?
16. Navigate the ongoing trends of multicultural learners?

Parents also report that they see diminished school engagement or excitement. Mom or other family members ask, "How was school today?" or "What did you learn today?" or "What did you do in school today?" The responses before third grade might be asking more questions or reconfirming what was taught: "We learned that sharks never sleep. Can that be true?" Once past third grade, however, "How was school today?" is met with "It was fine." Once past third grade: "What did you learn today?" is met with "Nothing." Once past third grade: "What did you do in school today?" is met with "Work." Or "Nothing" or "There was a fight."

One is apt to see students in third grade through high school hold conversations via phones even though they are sitting right next to each other. Schools have changed. Old school traditions/expectations were built on an agricultural seasonal calendar. Pedagogy was all about the sage on the stage talking "at" mainly nontalking students. The new school profiles expect learners to be engaged and ask questions as they build their own sense of understanding. New school educators must manage learning opportunities to use a myriad of resources and technology in authentic contexts to excite and engage today's learners. The backdrop of social media, conveniences, transportation, shopping malls, video games, and the many television channels are stiff competition for the minds of learners. Table I.1 suggests some of the more obvious changes from old school to new school.

Table I.1 School Changes

Old School—Traditional	New School—Innovative
Students did not question the educator	Why do we have to learn this? Students/learners are questioning, judging the authenticity, trying to figure out the value, seeking the relevance and personal connection to themselves
Educator was Sage on the Stage	Now the Educator is the Guide on the Side
No surveillance or armed security	Surveillance cameras and armed security
Looked it up in an encyclopedia or dictionary	Google It—Can the educator and the student trust internet information as honest and well-researched?
Purchased hardcover textbooks, used over and over	Textbooks are online—One does not have to wait for reprinting of texts because they are updated frequently
Chalkboards	Smart Boards and artificial intelligence
Socialized generally with kids in class or neighborhood or family	Socialization is expanded with the use of Instagram, X (formerly Twitter), WhatsApp, Facebook, TikTok, but always on the phone
Bulky computers	Lightweight and portable Chromebooks, iPads, Apple Pros, laptops, smartphones
The Classroom as the world	The World as the classroom
One phone in the office	Cell phones for everyone
Departmentalized, multi-educator environments in high school only	Departmentalized, multi-educator, and interdisciplinary subjects across all grades
One note professional development meetings	Differentiated professional development opportunities and experiences
Competition with a smattering of cooperation	Cooperation (group problem solving and team building) and competition
Immovable chairs in rows	Movable furniture
Snow days: no school	No missing school days: virtual school available online in any kind of weather and at any time
Diverse learners in separate classrooms	Diverse learners in least restrictive environments and/or in general education classes with modification and/or accommodations

(Continued)

Table I.1 (Continued)

Old School—Traditional	New School—Innovative
Principal, teachers, custodial staff, cafeteria lady	Many more specialists in schools: lunchroom staff, behavior interventionist, nurse, social worker, occupational therapist, speech therapist, reading specialist, math specialist, guidance counselors, assistant principals, district teams, guest speakers, bilingual teachers (who work with students who speak not only Spanish, but Urdu, Polish, Arabic, etc.), language interpreters
Mimeograph machines with purple goo	High-speed copiers and 3D printers
Neighborhood schools	Magnet schools with specialties like science, technology, engineering, and math (STEM), arts, math academies, college prep, Montessori, charter schools, and more

Why did the architect get fired for his library design?
Because it only had one story.

NOTES

1. A. Bandura, "Self-Efficacy: Toward a Unifying Theory of Behavioral Change." *Psychological Review* 84, no. 2 (1977): 241, https://doi.org/10.1037/0033-295X.84.2.191.

2. The single canon reference to this action being called a "salute" is in the episode "Journey to Babel," where Dr. McCoy asks Spock, "How does that Vulcan salute go?," *Star Trek* (season 2, episode 10), 1967.

3. Randi Weingarten, https://www.brainyquote.com/quotes/randi_weingarten_77644.

1

Metacognition/Executive Functioning for Both Educator and Learner
Using Questions

Once you learn to question, you will start to learn."

—Abhijit Naskar, *Sleepless for Society*[1]

Quite often, teachers (professional educators) are not treated like other professionals:

1. An unhealthy person doesn't affect a doctor's salary ... but low test scores can result in a pay cut for teachers.
2. Dentists aren't blamed when their patients don't brush or floss ... but it's the teacher's fault when students don't complete their work.
3. Pilots aren't forced to fly into a hurricane ... but teachers are expected to continue "business" as usual despite countless hurdles.
4. A chef isn't expected to feed diners who aren't at a restaurant ... but teachers are sometimes expected to pass students who don't come to school.
5. The public views skilled laborers as irreplaceable ... but then believe any warm body can lead a classroom.

Objectives:

a. Suggested Educator Tool—"Check Yourself Before You Wreck Yourself"

(See tables 1.2 and 1.3 for Educator Planning Tool Samples for ELA and Math Learning Standard [Point of View and Algebra])
b. Suggested Educator Tool to Manage Basic Prerequisites and Missing Foundational Knowledge around the Learning Standards
c. Suggested Learner Tool to Encourage Metacognitive Strategies to Examine the Learners' Developing Knowledge of How They Learn How They Learn
d. Some Sample Questions of the Day

SUGGESTED EDUCATOR TOOL—"CHECK YOURSELF BEFORE YOU WRECK YOURSELF"

"To travel is to take a journey into yourself" (Danny Kaye).

An educator is a "trained" professional who creates the blueprints (lesson/unit plans). Educators don't know everything. They must review what is to be taught. They determine what learner outcomes may be desired or expected. They must figure strategies to motivate their learners to be interested in any learning episode. They must be intentional to help the learner use their thinking, seeing, and hearing to maximize learning potential. The authors feel that unit planning and/or project-based learning can be beneficial. Unit planning and/or project-based learning support an educator's metacognitive thinking about analyzing what is to be taught.

Most teachers (professional educators) have philosophical notions about how they learn as learners and how to deliver instructional content and skills. Here is a quick review of those popular philosophies of learning.

Behaviorism suggests one learns when outside stimuli is presented to change behaviors. Behaviorism presupposes that the mind is an empty vessel and is influenced by repeated reinforcement. What kind of questions might the behaviorist ask? It's called "conditioning." Classical conditioning suggests that the learner/educator connect two stimuli to get to the desired behaviors and/or learning objectives. Operant conditioning suggests consequences control responses. The behaviorist uses questions to get the desired response, drills, reinforcement, and regular reviews.

Cognitivism suggests that one processes and organizes in their mind new knowledge that may be presented. The theory suggests that one passively processes information and creates memory.

Constructivism says that one learns new knowledge by linking new knowledge with previously learned knowledge/experience.

Additionally, there are new learning theories that have emerged: *Humanism* (Maslow,[2] Rogers[3]) and *Connectivism* (Siemens, Downes[4]). Humanism says that everyone functions under a hierarchy of needs.

Humanism is about environment; if the environment is right (safe) and needs are met, then one can learn. Connectivism suggests that learners learn new knowledge as they "connect the dots" of their roles, obligations, hobbies, goals, people, and so on. All educators/learners use combinations of these educational learning theories as they co-construct instruction with their learners.

THINK/DISCUSSION BREAK I

Think about how you learned to drive, or cook, or ride a bicycle—the emotions, the knowledge base, the practice, the generalization of skills to other vehicles. How can each (or combinations) of these learning theories be applied to your experience?

Table 1.1 Suggested Planner for an Educator: Select the Learning Standards before Learning Episodes Are Taught/Delivered

	Known	Questions	Variables, Activities, Resources
What is the foundation of the standard or core concepts (curriculum)? What are the parts?			
Why teach this? How is this connected to life?			
What's the logic of what is to be comprehended?			
What is the necessary vocabulary?			
What possible applications of the standard can be connected or integrated to other learnings (writings, speaking, persuading, research, etc.)?			
SCHOOL TASK RELATED			
What research, tools, material, anecdotes, metaphors, analogies, digital support, or internet sources may make this standard more digestible?			
What instructional strategies might work with this standard?			VAKT—<u>V</u>isual, <u>A</u>uditory, <u>K</u>inesthetic, and <u>T</u>actile

Table 1.2 Example of Educator Planning Tool Sample*

	Known	Questions	Variables, Activities, Resources
What is the foundation of the standard (curriculum)?	All authors have a purpose to connect with audience: persuade, inform, and entertain (PIE)	What are the essential questions? What is the author's purpose? What are possible literary techniques to demonstrate POV?	Ability to identify, understand, interpret, evaluate, create, compute, and/or communicate
Why teach this? How is this connected to life?	Reading is fundamental for managing lifelong learning: voting, driving, paying bills, understanding commercials, contracts, taxes; participation with others and self-aggrandizement; choosing entertainment genres; equity, etc.	What lifelong situations depend on persuasive savvy? Depend on information savvy? Depend on entertainment savvy?	Connecting POV to personal decisions: health, finances, quality of life, employment, specialized training, family life
What's the logic of what is to be comprehended?	Distinguishing authors' literary techniques as they describe character, plot, setting, phenomena	How does one find the main ideas with supporting details—explicitly and implicitly? What are the themes of the story?	Examining the beginning, middle, and end for logical flow. Examines the relationships among the characters
What is the necessary vocabulary?	Character, plot, setting, inference, main idea, details, POV	What vocabulary words in the various literary pieces may be challenging?	Level of skill for: • Decoding words • Oral fluency, prosody or rhythm, and flow • Comprehension and contextual clues

What possible applications of the standard can be connected or integrated to other learnings (writings, speaking, persuading, research, etc.)? SCHOOL TASK RELATED	• Making decisions on multiple-choice test questions • Creating a list of ideas for an argument or debate • Knowing when to do research for a science project • Understanding and executing a rubric • Responding to writing prompts • Using context clues		Compare and contrast author's point of view and the reader's point of view
What research, tools, material, anecdotes, metaphors, analogies, digital support, or internet sources may make this standard more digestible?	Digital Tools: Videos, YouTube, Kahn Academy, BrainPop, Kahoot!, Mentimeter Mnemonic—PIE Literary Themes: power, friendship, family, identity, loneliness, free will (vs. fate), hope, love, war, childhood, coming of age, environment and climate change	How can POV (inference) be connected to persuade, inform, and entertain (PIE) in writing a letter or dialog for a play, speaking or debating around a subject, acting a part in a play? How do certain songs persuade, inform, or entertain?	Scaffolding from known stories to new literary passages
What instructional strategies might work with this standard?	• Fables • Myths • Poetry • Tall stories • Short stories	What is the moral or teaching that the author wanted the reader to understand?	Television script samples of the same items (like fast food, toothpaste, news programs)
Other notes	Writing; Journal writing or Recording voice about POV	What inputs? What activities? What outputs? What outcomes?	
Miscellany—Cultural Competency; DEI		What grammatical rules, protocols, structures must be taught? What spelling rules should be highlighted? What cultural lens may understand the difference between mirror books and window books?	
Collegial Support		What does grade-level meeting or reading specialist suggest for this concept?	

For third grade language arts—Standard is to distinguish their own point of view (POV) from that of the narrator or the characters in the story.

Table 1.3 Learning Standard Sample: High School Algebra

	Known	Questions	Variables, Activities, Resources
What is the foundation of the standard (curriculum)?	Solving for the unknown Equal sign is one-to-one correspondence	Why does X or a letter stand in the place of an unknown? What does more mean? What does less mean? Does equal always look the same on both sides of the equation?	
Why teach this? How is this connected to life?	What happens when things break down in one's home or apartment or dorm room?		
What's the logic of what is to be comprehended?	Every number is a sign, a coefficient, and a variable	What does 3 mean in the following: 3,000; 3; -3; $3.00; .003; 3rd?	Place value
What is the necessary vocabulary?	Equal sign; associative property; distributive property; signed numbers; base ten system		
What possible applications of the standard can be connected or integrated to other learnings (writings, speaking, persuading, research, etc.)?			
What research, tools, material, anecdotes, metaphors, analogies, digital support, or internet sources may make this standard more digestible?			
What instructional strategies might work with this standard?			
Other notes			
Miscellany			
Collegial Support			

A SUGGESTED EDUCATOR TOOL TO MANAGE BASIC PREREQUISITES AND MISSING FOUNDATIONAL KNOWLEDGE AROUND THE LEARNING STANDARDS

A solid foundation is crucial for the stability, capacity, and structural integrity of a building. Without a proper foundation, the entire structure is at risk, and it may not be safe or suitable for occupancy. Building codes and engineering standards are in place to ensure that foundations are constructed correctly to support the weight of the walls, floors, and roofs. Indeed, there is a strong analogy between a building's foundation and the educational foundation for learners. Just as a solid foundation is vital for the stability and integrity of a building, a strong foundation is essential for learners. It forms the basis for their future learning and development, ensuring that they have the necessary knowledge and skills to succeed in their academic journey and beyond.

Foundational knowledge includes basic literacy, numeracy, and transferable skills. When an educator is focusing on learner outcomes, there is usually a disconnect of missing foundation knowledge between old and new impending learnings. School seems far away from adulthood, but what is learned affects how each learner deals with the realities of human life and the choices they make. It is critical to support those skills necessary by using strategies that promote independence and critical thinking to enable the learner to build their own knowledge.

Educators frequently report that when they are teaching multiplication of three-digit numbers their learners don't know the multiplication facts. Other learners present evidence that they don't know punctuation, grammar, or syntax when writing in their journals. How can an educator find out the missing foundational knowledge as they plan and scaffold to new learnings?

Every learner has had different experiences from their classmates. Some have never been out of their neighborhood, while others have traveled to other countries around the world. Those experiences must be tapped to ensure that the CIA (curriculum, instruction, and assessment) investigates learner readiness to understand and apply the concepts and skills to be taught. The curriculum is the path or the ideas of what learners should know and be able to do by a certain grade level. Learners in any grade, usually, fall in the high, middle, and low ranges of those specific "grade" levels. Educator efficacy is quite often determined by what each learner knows and is able to do (learning standards). Understanding those missing "links" helps with grouping and differentiation. For example, an Illinois learning standard says all fifth graders can: "Use combined knowledge of all letter-sound correspondences, syllabication patterns, and morphology (e.g., roots and affixes) to read accurately unfamiliar multisyllabic words in context and out of context)." This is a vital skill in reading bills, letters, memos and other writing, applying for a job, or creating a business. Breaking down the nonsense word *seligrandom* is helpful when deciphering clothing catalogue language such as packable, innovative, breathability, and abrasion-resistant. Using real-time artifacts like a clothing catalogue may be an additional "textbook."

Suggested Pretest Strategies for Educators

Certainly, reviewing academic language and mathematical terms is valuable in education. It's important for educators to bridge the gap between everyday language and academic vocabulary to ensure that learners can transfer their skills to other disciplines. Relatable examples, like equating a character in a story to a person discussed in academic discourse, can help learners learn the common parlance (vocabulary) that are easily transferable to English Language Arts stories in social studies, biographies, research articles, theatrical plays, and sports games. Effective teaching often involves making complex ideas more accessible to learners. See the following for examples (may be used as occasional bell ringers) of some ways that might get at what is missing:

1. For character, setting, and plot—ask learners to list characters and/or setting and/or plot from a story you read together and where a copy of the book is available for all learners.
2. For inference, ask learners to infer from the sentences below what they think will happen or what comes next or is the person who is speaking mad or glad or sad. For upper grades, play a speech from a famous person and ask if they can infer meaning.
3. Ask learners to copy the five sentences you write on the board and ask them to identify (circle) all the punctuation marks.
4. Ask learners to circle capital letters and square small letters in a written sentence or two.
5. Ask learners to look at two animals (or symbols or concepts) and compare and contrast them (e.g., frog and rabbit, dog and rabbit, snake and panda, Na and CL, sine and cosine, circumference and radius, triangle and octagon).
6. Ask learners to write numbers from one to one hundred, or identify which number would come next in a number series.
7. Ask the learner to identify among a group of fractions which is the proper fraction, improper fraction, and the mixed fraction, dividends, quotients, minuends, addends.
8. Which property best demonstrates the following equations?
    a. $A + B = B + A$
    b. $A \times B = B \times A$
    c. $(3 + 5) \times 6 = 18 + 30 = 8 \times 6$

Foundational knowledge is the bridge connecting prior knowledge to new knowledge. Learners learn from educators and their classmates. Educators may ask learners to help get the answers to the aforementioned questions by sharing thought processes with their neighbor. Bell ringers are a good source of finding out the strength of foundational knowledge before teaching such topics as fractions, positive and negative numbers, or literary styles. Teaching learners to look for the key words in instructions or directions is necessary to move forward. Think-alouds, modeling, and graphic organizers can support learning to connect what is new with old content and skills.

The proverbial saying "The greatest helping hand is at the end of your own arm" speaks to the independence, ownership, participation, and responsibility that is a goal for learners.

Yes, using notebooks to house the information (vocabulary, step by steps, graphic organizers) will help learners to become more independent. Adults use notes to themselves all the time—grocery lists, bills to be paid, collecting tax evidence, packing for trips, and so on. So can educators analyze past records, statewide test results, data collection, formative and summative assessments, as well as observations to understand their students' strengths and weaknesses. Collected student interest inventories can be used to motivate participation in learning episodes. Administering a pretest before a learning episode and repeating it at the end can help identify areas where learners may need reteaching. This data-driven approach allows educators to anticipate what needs to be retaught, where it is related to vocabulary, specific skills, or foundational knowledge gaps and then tailor their instruction accordingly.

The educator has two planning tools to understand their own knowledge of the concepts and skills to be taught and what foundational knowledge is needed for a concept and skill (standard) to be minimally introduced, developed, and taught.

SUGGESTED LEARNER TOOL TO ENCOURAGE METACOGNITIVE STRATEGIES TO EXAMINE THE LEARNERS' DEVELOPING KNOWLEDGE OF HOW THEY LEARN HOW THEY LEARN

Most educators are familiar with the organizational tool: KWL. The acronym is K—what do I know; W—what do I want to know; and L—what have I learned. Students can employ this system to examine their own thinking about a learning episode or series of episodes. After an educator presents the concepts and skills to be learned and presents the tasks, the learner can use this tool to examine what is known, what they would like to know, and what has been learned. This tool may be used as a solo task or developed in a small group.

Table 1.4 Missing Concepts and Skills Foundation Tool for an Educator to Use to Support Reteaching Using the English Language Arts Learning Standards around a Point of View

Standard	Minimal	Developing and distinguishing	Activities to build memory; Hands-on application of concept/skills
What is the standard? e.g., POV (point of view)	Basic concepts and skills needed to understand the standard	Understanding essential vocabulary to use in describing the phenomena—Key Words	Increasing brain plasticity for short-term and long-term memory
Foundational knowledge—Scaffolding previous learnings including vocabulary	Can comprehend familiar stories to bridge the gap between the reader and the author	Theme, point of view, first person (I, we, me), second person (you), third person (he, she, it, they, them), narrator, author	Making crossword puzzles, meditation, visualizing, socializing, draw, make a flowchart
Engagement strategies	Can dissect "Little Red" and the "Three Little Pigs" to discover the authors' POV	Co-construct worksheets with all students, matching with questions and answers for review	Small group contests to determine first, second, third person narrators Student journaling small stories—recorded or written Listening to stories on tape
How, what, who, where, when, and why questions to ask . . .	Who is the author, illustrator, theme, characters, plot, purpose, setting, beginning, middle and end?	Is when the story takes place necessary to understand POV? What could be the connection between the theme and the author?	What does the internet tell the reader about the author's life? How might the author's life contribute to their POV?
Material needed	Finding amazing stories from movies, television, etc. Grade-level story—fiction Grade-level story—nonfiction News article	Co-creating a protocol by which to dissect and connect the author's POV to the narrator or the reader	Journal POV evaluations or critiques of at least five stories

Table 1.4 (Continued)

Digital connections	Listening and/or looking at familiar stories Seeing the same story over and over to get concepts and skills	Reading a variety of Google entries around the ideas of POV	Comparing opinion pieces around author's themes and POV
Formative assessments	Exit surveys	Case study discussions	Co-constructed final assessments
Summative assessments	Journaling concept, skills, and themes around POV	Chapter test	Analysis of opinion pieces with student POV

Again, the educator is the architect or designer that helps develop the learner's personal quest for learning how they learn how they learn. The five senses admit information but for life—eyes, ears, smell, touch, and taste. Those senses are tools for learning. Sometimes a sour lemon candy given when teaching a learning standard around POV aids a discussion on how the tension of sour and sweet makes one remember the author and narrator or the theme and the chosen setting.

Ask yourself as an educator—How do you best learn when presented with some information like assembling something you bought from IKEA? Some complete the IKEA project reading the directions, others from looking at the pictures, and still others from hearing and seeing a YouTube video. Learners, generally, learn visually, auditorily, and kinesthetically by touch, reading, and writing. The educator's lesson episode must try to present the concepts and skills incorporating all the aforementioned styles.

There are other components to learning that must be considered:

1. Does one like to work in a group or solo?
2. Does one like to feel they belong and are cared about by the educator?
3. Does one feel like making a mistake is permissible?
4. Does one feel like feedback helps lead to better understanding?
5. Does one feel independence in developing mastery of concepts and skills? "I learned this by myself."
6. Does one believe they can learn what is being taught?

Table 1.5 is a tool for educators to develop how learners learn how they learn. This tool can be used as an exit survey for some lessons. When time permits, collect these surveys and see if you begin to see patterns of learning and patterns for pedagogy.

Chapter 1

Table 1.5 Educators Learn How Learners Learn Episode Exit Survey

Learning Episode: What was the concept taught? (and/or skill)			Date:	
	Somewhat	or	Mostly	Comments—write or talk
Did seeing the models make sense to me?				
Did listening about the concept or skill make sense to me?				
Did reading the materials available make sense to me?				
Did writing or rewriting help me remember what I was learning?				
Did learning in a group make it easier to learn the concept?				
Was this information fun to learn?				
Was this concept similar to other information learned?				What other information?
Am I still struggling with the concept or skill?	No		Yes	I think I need help with . . .

SOME SAMPLE QUESTIONS OF THE DAY

1. If . . . , How Questions:
    If sharks never sleep, how do they rest?
    If zero times zero equals zero, how do zeros function in numbers like 30, 400, $10.00?
    If 6^3 is equal to 216, how does 6 times 3 only equal 18?
    If John has $40.18, how can he possibly pay for his new computer that costs $520.00?
    If I am thinking of winning the lottery, how do I make that happen?

2. If . . . , Then Questions:
    If I can make a loaf of bread with five ingredients, then how many loaves of bread with ten ingredients?
    If I wrote ten pages every day for a book, then how many pages can I write for sixteen days? How many pages if I can only write for five days?
    If Cinderella did not have a fairy godmother, then how could she go to ball anyway?

3. Why Questions (researchable and fun-filled):
    Why is the sky blue?
    Why can't scientists determine the color of dinosaurs?
    Why is garbage collected every day?
    Why are we using the same water that the cavemen used?
4. What Questions:
    What time is it in London right now?
    What can you make with string?
    What can you drink or eat to make you healthy?
5. Comparison Questions:
    How is a paperclip and a pencil alike?
    How is a car and a pair of shoes similar?
    How is a phone and a coffee pot similar?
6. Content Recyclable Questions:
    What three things do you know about fractions?
    What nine things do you know about the parts of a book?
    What is strange but true about punctuation marks?
7. Metacognitive Questions:
    How do I study spelling words to improve my test scores?
    Where is my frustration with understanding decimals?
    What and why is it my best subject?
8. If I Ruled the World Questions:
    If I won the lottery for $1,000,000, what would I spend it on and why?
    If I could study how to cure some diseases, which ones are the ones I'd study about?
    If I could eat anything I wanted every day (and it not be harmful to my health), what would it be and why?
    If I could go back in time, what would I fix?
9. Curious Questions:
    Why is the shelf life of some foods so important to consider and throw away if expired?
    What are the ingredients in my favorite candy bar and what do they mean?
    What's so fun about my favorite video game besides being fun?
    What buying decisions do rich people make to make them so rich?
    Why do people pay taxes?
    What do I pay taxes on?
10. Ethereal Questions:
    What does it mean to make a sacrifice?
    What is love?
    What does it mean to care about something?

11. Relationship Questions:
    What does it mean to be a friend?
    How do you choose a friend?
    What does it mean do trust a friend?
    How do I know that I am loved?
    What does it mean to trust your "gut"?
    Who do I talk to on the phone a lot and why?
    What do I love about my family?
    What is a hater?
12. Persistence Type Questions:
    What have I finished?
    What do you do every day that you complete no matter what?
    What can I cook from start to finish—from ingredients to the plate?
    Where do I get help if I can't finish my homework?
    How do I try and figure what class or homework assignments are required to complete the tasks?
13. Reliance Type Questions:
    What do people (friends, neighbors, family) count on me for?
    What can you depend on me forever and a day for?
    Who do I depend on?
    Does the weather report determine what I wear when I go outside? Why or why not?
14. Skill Questions:
    What sports am I good at? How do I know?
    What are strengths in school? How do I know?
    Can I throw a birthday party for a friend? How can I prove that I can throw such a party?
    What do I read *every day*? What do I learn from what I read?
15. Techy Questions:
    What gadgets do I use all the time?
    How much time am I in front of my Chromebook every day?
    How much time do I spend playing video games?
    Do I have an iPad, iPhone, or Android? Who bought it for me? How much did it cost? What if it breaks down? Where do I go to get it fixed?
    What are my favorite games and why?
16. Health Questions:
    How much do I weigh? How tall am I?
    What health issues have I experienced?
    How do my scars tell my story?
    What does it mean to eat healthy?
    What is my exercise routine?

17. Planning Questions;
    How do I plan what I am going to wear tomorrow?
    What am I always waiting for?
18. Mad Glad Questions;
    What makes me mad?
    What makes me glad?
    What do I do when I get really mad?
    What do I share when I'm really glad?
19. Prediction Questions:
    What do you think will happen next?
    If that was you in the story, what might you do to keep yourself safe?
    What inferences can you make to guess what will happen next?

NOTES

1. A. Naskar, *Sleepless for Society*, 2020, https://goodreads.com.
2. A. Maslow (1962), "Humanistic Approach in Psychology (Humanism)," https://www.simplypsychology.org/humanistic.html.
3. C. Rogers (1959), "A Theory of Therapy, Personality, and Interpersonal Relationships, as Developed in the Client-Centered Framework," *Psychology: A Study of Science*, 3, 184–256.
4. G. Siemens, "Connectivism: Learning as Network Creation," 2004, http://www.asted.oeg/LC/2005/1105_Siemens.htm; S. Downes, "An Introduction to Connective Knowledge," 2005, http://mediarep.org/entities/bookpart/57553029-32a-49a1-8b18-30d9d14afc72/full.

2

✢

Teaching the Art of Questioning for Both Educator and Learner

Judge a man by his questions rather than his answers.

—Voltaire

Objectives:

a. Educator Sample Questions around Lesson Planning
b. Educator Sample Questions to Ask Students (Bloom's Taxonomy)
c. Educator Strategies to Teach Students to Ask Questions
d. Managing Student Questions

EDUCATOR SAMPLE LESSON/UNIT PLANNING QUESTIONS FOR ANALYSIS AND REFLECTION (TOWARD TEACHER EFFICACY)

Before an instructional lesson or episode, here are some questions to use as a guide:

1. What objectives, standards, skill, content, goals, and disciplines are being taught?
2. Does the lesson demonstrate at least two ways to show the objective, goal, concept, skill, discipline?
3. What concepts are essential?
4. What skills are fundamental?
5. What learner assumptions are to be considered?

6. What opportunities have been made for learner's voice and choice?
7. What is the intersection between the educator, learner, and concept/skill to be taught?
8. What learning evidence is expected of the learner?
9. What are lesson aspects that challenge the learner?

During the instructional lesson:

1. Do the learners recognize the objectives, standards, skills, content, goals, disciplines being taught?
2. Are the learners engaged?
3. Are there gaps in essential concepts or learners' existent knowledge?
4. Are there gaps in fundamental knowledge (like the "automatic" recall of the multiplication facts or "logical" kinds of structures like if . . . then; or creating schemas or algorithms/formulas to manage complex information)?
5. What kind of learner questions (beyond recall) are generated?
6. What metacognitive strategies are used to guide and organize the learners' thinking and reasoning around the concept and skill?
7. Have the learners been challenged and guided?

After the instructional lesson:

1. How did the lesson feel to the educator?
2. How did the lesson feel for the learner (as gleaned from exit slips or journal entries)?
3. Which practices did the educator think were successful? Unsuccessful?
4. What did the learners' behavior reveal about the skills/concepts learned?
5. Did the formative and/or summative (learner responses) reflect educator intentions?
6. What other "signs" should the educator look for to improve instruction?

Synthesizing: Educator and Learner might answer some of the following questions together:

1. What concepts and skills were learned?
2. What concepts and skills are connected to what one already knows?
3. What was I thinking and feeling as the lesson progressed?
4. What was of personal interest?
5. What did I learn that I might share with someone else?
6. What words did I see for the first time?

7. What was familiar? Unfamiliar?
8. What must be reviewed? Practiced?
9. What concepts and skills did I learn to help me learn other concepts/skills? What concepts and skills may transfer to other lessons?

EDUCATOR SAMPLE QUESTIONS TO ASK STUDENTS

Strategy I: Bloom's Taxonomy offers ingenious question starters that all educators can use. See table 2.1.

Lorin Anderson and David Krathwohl have suggested question prompts for designing student questions during learning episodes.[1]

Remembering—Knowledge

Recall or recognize information and ideas.
The teacher should:

- Present information about the subject to the student
- Ask questions that require the student to recall the information presented
- Provide verbal or written texts about the subject that can be answered by recalling the information the student has learned

Questioning prompts:

What do you remember about _____?	Where is (are) _____?
How would you define _____?	Which one _____?
How would you identify _____?	Who was _____?
How would you recognize _____?	Why did _____?
What would you choose _____?	What is (are) _____?
Describe what happens when _____?	When did _____?
How is (are) _____?	How would you outline _____?
List the _____ in order.	

Understanding—Comprehension

Understand the main idea of material heard, viewed, or read. Interpret or summarize the ideas in your own words.
The teacher should:

- Ask questions that the student can answer in his or her own words by stating facts or by identifying the main idea
- Give tests based on classroom instruction

Table 2.1 Bloom's Ingenious Question Asking Strategies and Tasks

	Suggested Task Language	Kinds of Questions for Students
I. REMEMBERING	List, identify, cite, recognize, locate, label, find, state, define, reproduce, quote, select, match, draw, retrieve, show, tell, describe, memorize, recall, write	Who? What? Where? Why? How? Which? When?
II. UNDERSTANDING	Classify, compare, explain, extend, illustrate, implement, infer, interpret, outline, relate, rephrase, show, summarize, use, translate	Summarize? Outline? Derive by reasoning? Conclude? Examine? Fulfill?
III. APPLYING	Apply, build, calculate, change, choose, construction, demonstrate, develop, dramatize, experiment, employ, execute, complete, illustrate, interview, model, organize, plan, practice, produce, select, solve, utilize	Put into effect? Mold? Make something different? Build by putting parts together? Accomplish? Systematize? Cause? Manufacture? Habit?
IV. ANALYZING	Appraise, assume, categorize, classify, compare, conclude, contrast, debate, differentiate, discover, dissect, distinguish, divide, estimate, examine, explain, figure, function, inspect, investigate, resolve, scrutinize, simplify, separate, test	Hypothesize? Compute? Set apart? Assign meaning? Arrange by classes or groups? Undertake? Make plain? Perform? Show proof?
V. EVALUATING	Argue, assess, check, choose, convince, critique, decide, defend, determine, discuss, estimate, evaluate, explain, influence, interpret, judge, justify, measure, perceive, prioritize, prove, rank, rate, recommend, survey, verify	Select? Persuade? Cajole? Determine value? Settle an argument? Use evidence? Judge? Prove? Truth? Competition? Estimate? Hold as an opinion?
VI. CREATING	Start, shape, author, create, fabricate, invent, propose, fashion, formulate, combine, perform, forecast, manage, reorganize, collect, compose, design, devise, make	Originate? Forecasting? Intending? Take charge of something? Assemble? Unite?

Questioning prompts:

How would you compare _____?	How would you identify _____?
Contrast _____?	How can you describe _____?
How would you clarify the meaning _____?	Will you restate _____?
How would you differentiate between ____?	Elaborate on _____.
How would you generalize _____?	What would happen if _____?
How would you express _____?	What is the main idea of _____?
What can you infer from _____?	What can you say about _____?
What did you observe _____?	

Applying—Application

Apply an abstract idea in a concrete situation to solve a problem or relate it to prior experience.
The teacher should:

- Provide opportunities for the student to use ideas, theories, or problem-solving techniques and apply them to new situations
- Review the student's work to ensure that he or she is using problem-solving techniques independently
- Provide questions that require the student to define and solve problems

Questioning prompts:

What actions would you take to perform ____?	How would you modify _____?
How would you develop ____ to present ____?	How could you develop _____?
What other way would you choose _____?	Why does _____ work?
What would the result be if _____?	How would you alter _____ to _____?
How would you demonstrate _____?	What examples can you find that ____?
How would you present _____?	How would you solve _____?
How would you change _____?	

Analyzing—Analysis

Break down a concept or idea into parts and show relationships among the parts.
The teacher should:

- Allow time for students to examine concepts and ideas and to break them down into basic parts
- Require students to explain why they chose a certain problem-solving technique and why the solution worked

Questioning prompts:

How can you classify ____ according to ____?	What can you infer _____?
How can you compare the different parts ____?	What ideas validate _____?
What explanation do you have for _____?	How would you explain _____?
How is _____ connected to _____?	What can you point out about _____?
Discuss the pros and cons of _____.	What is the problem with _____?
How can you sort the parts _____?	Why do you think_____?
What is the analysis of _____?	

Evaluating—Evaluation

Make informed judgments about the value of ideas or materials. Use standards and criteria to support opinions and views.

The teacher should:

- Provide opportunities for students to make judgments based on appropriate criteria.
- Have students demonstrate that they can judge, critique, or interpret processes, materials, methods, and so on using standards and criteria.

Questioning prompts:

What criteria would you use to assess ____?	What is your opinion of _____?
What data was used to evaluate _____?	How could you verify _____?
What choice would you have made_____?	What information would you use to prioritize ___?
How would you determine the facts _____?	
What is the most important _____?	Rate the _____.
What would you suggest _____?	Rank the importance of _____.
How would you grade _____?	Determine the value of _____.

Creating—Synthesis

Bring together parts of knowledge to form a whole and build relationships for new situations.

The teacher should:

- Provide opportunities for students to assemble parts of knowledge into a whole using creative thinking and problem solving
- Require students to demonstrate that they can combine concepts to build new ideas for new situations

Questioning prompts:

What alternative would you suggest for ___?	What changes would you make to revise___?
How would you explain the reason _____?	How would you portray _____?
How would you generate a plan to _____?	Devise a way to _____.
What could you invent _____?	How would you compile the facts for _____?
What facts can you gather _____?	How would you elaborate on the reason___?
Predict the outcome if _____.	How would you improve _____?
What would happen if _____?	What learner outcomes are expected? _____.

Bloom's Taxonomy (revised 2001) uses a pedagogical classification system of educational learning objectives that go from complex and to specific. Generally, educators ask *remembering* questions during instruction: Who? What? Where? Why? How? Which? and/or When? To assess a most basic *understanding* of the standard taught, an educator may ask for an outline, a summary, or a conclusion. The level of *applying* is a little more intricate with questions or directed tasks that involve building, illustrating, selecting, utilizing, choosing (multiple-choice questions), modeling, and/or organizing.

Bloom's levels of *analyzing, evaluating,* and *creating* are more specific and require both learner and educator to put more of their unique self into those levels. When asked to analyze (appraise, compare, classify, contrast, or conclude), the learner or educator has to "own" their actions. When asked to evaluate (argue, convince, influence, rank, rate, verify), the learner or educator has to participate with others to manage the discourse. When asked to create (shape, invent, fabricate, compose, design, make, or fashion), the learner or educator interprets their self-understanding of the concept/skills taught.

EDUCATOR STRATEGIES TO TEACH STUDENTS TO ASK QUESTIONS

When educators ask questions of learners, it assures communication. Learners process and practice the language of information.

Strategy I: That old game Twenty Questions is a good way to encourage learners to ask questions. Learners are presented with a closed box with something in it that must be guessed by asking questions that can be answered yes or no. Whoever guesses correctly gets a small prize.

Strategy II: Using class books or a small article, ask learners to note the question mark as a signal for a question. Have learners list questions from the book or article. Then have learners do mini biographies of their classmates or celebrities by listing questions they may ask to find out information about their classmate or celebrity.

Strategy III: Play class Jeopardy to answer a statement with a question. Play a Kahoot! game to ask questions with choice answers. Then have learners create a class Jeopardy game for either another grade level or the same grade level around a concept and/or skill. Have learners develop a Kahoot! game to review a lesson taught.

Strategy IV: Have learners and educators co-construct formative assessments around what has been learned.

Strategy V: All students look at television; find out what their popular shows and/or streamed movies are and ask them to write down at least three questions that one of the characters asked; include quiz shows and mysteries.

Strategy VI: Surround students with real artifacts—receipts from groceries (basic numeracy); garment tags (why are tags necessary); candy wrappers (compare ingredients, decode words, pronunciation, syllabication); instructional manuals; empty cold and headache packages; several brands of the same product. Using familiar artifacts, collecting them supports initial question-asking forays. What is this receipt for? What extra ingredients does Bayer aspirin have that Advil does not?

Strategy VII: Use contests for grouping and conversation. How are a paperclip and a pencil alike? What is the best thing you ever ate?

Strategy VIII: To get the best bang from the myriad of charts around the room, have learners make up question and answer tests from the charts posted, where the answers are obvious. There is an opportunity to make this a contest. For example, one posted chart may have the definition of a noun is a person, place, animal, or thing. The question developed by the class or small group might be, What part of speech is a person? The next learner in line must go to the chart and point to the answer.

* * *

An educator may use anchor charts posted around the room or ask learners to archive information in notebooks (per discipline) to foster independence. These practices provide opportunities for learners to build their own knowledge. For some learners, get them started with "copying" notes or beginning a graphic organizer, where they fill in the missing word or concept in their own words. Allow learners to use their notes, anchor charts, or textbooks as they take either the formative or summative assessments. It is more valuable for learners to research the answers than to have the educator provide answers. Having a common goal to pass an assessment or answer a question posed helps in extending the life of a unit/lesson.

Group work can also get learners to communicate their understanding with their peers. An educator could facilitate joint notetaking, joint assessments, joint reviews of written work or numerical computations. Providing opportunities for learners to practice "each one teach one" can support peer-assisted learning. There are good reasons to use calculators at times, as well as internet support in certain situations. Learners should have the opportunity to have phonics, multiplication tables, or anything that might sustain the "flow" or rhythm of the lesson when there is missing foundational knowledge. Learners should have the opportunity to review, revisit, recalculate, and reflect on their work. Learning from mistakes (with correction) is more memorable than easy successes.

Learners should have the opportunity to reflect on their learnings. Ask questions at the beginning, during, and end of significant learning episodes that include: What new words did I learn? What can I do with information in real life, or Why do I need to know this? What parts are still unclear to me? Where do I think I need help or tutoring?

Some techniques educators may employ are real-life case studies to stimulate critical thinking:

1. Sonja (ten years old) needs to pack for her upcoming trip to her grandmother's house which is a five-hour drive. She'll be staying with her grandmother for five days. Pack her suitcase with the essential clothing and toiletries and explain why. Use a class novel like *A Smart Girl's Guide: Travel: Everything You Need to Know about Adventuring Near and Far*[2] and employ the words that the main character chooses to describe the tasks.
2. Sam is shopping for apartment furniture. He must make a list of the stores in his neighborhood that sell furniture and those he can find on the internet. He must purchase a bed and a chair, and his budget is $350. If he can't carry the bed and the chair, he must account for delivery charges. Help him out, choose the best deal.
3. Rewrite the ending to a familiar story.
4. Jose and Latrice are going to Alaska, what would they need to take on a three-day trip to see the famous glaciers?

NOTES

1. L. W. Anderson and D. R. Krathwohl, eds., *A Taxonomy for Learning, Teaching, and Assessing: A Revision of Bloom's Taxonomy of Educational Outcomes: Complete Edition* (New York: Longman, 2001).

2. Aubre Andrus, *A Smart Girl's Guide: Travel: Everything You Need to Know about Adventuring Near and Far*. American Girl Wellbeing. Illustrated by Stevie Lewis (Middleton, WI: American Girl Publishing, 2019).

3

✣

Technology as a Useful Tool to Answer and Explore Questions

Technology costs money. If educators are not trained (and knowledgeable of software available) in software use (from managing data to choosing what information to use to engage and/or enhance learning episodes), then technology can expose learners to threats, bullying, harassment, and the like. Technology can help learners/educators be empathetic (recognizing and appreciating similarities and differences), manage stress and control impulses when faced with obstacles, learn how to establish and maintain healthy relationships, resist conflict and social pressure, and know that with decisions, there are consequences. The purpose of this chapter is to create a safe online learning environment for internet safety.

Objectives:

a. Social Emotional Learning
b. Internet Safety
c. Authenticity
d. AI—the Elephant in the Room

SOCIAL EMOTIONAL LEARNING

Social and emotional learning (SEL) as a curriculum has emerged to mitigate activities that undermine the teaching and learning climate. Are educators creating environments/atmospheres for learners to feel secure and confident as they express themselves and take on challenges to try something new?

Creating a safe internet environment for learners in classrooms and managing misinformation involves a multifaceted approach:

1. Educate Learners: Teach learners critical thinking and digital literacy skills to help them evaluate information sources and identify misinformation.
2. Content Filtering: Implement content filtering and firewall solutions to block inappropriate or harmful content.
3. Educator Training: Provide ongoing professional development for educators on digital literacy and safe internet use.
4. Trusted Resources: Encourage educators to use trusted educational websites and resources. Government and academic websites are often reliable.
5. Fact-Checking Tools: Promote the use of fact-checking websites and tools to verify information.
6. Parental Involvement: Involve parents in internet safety discussions and provide resources for them to monitor and guide their children's online activities.
7. Community Guidelines: Emphasize the importance of respecting community guidelines and reporting inappropriate content.
8. Digital Citizenship: Teach students about responsible online behavior and the consequences of cyberbullying and misinformation.
9. Open Communication: Foster open communication between educators, learners, and parents about internet safety concerns.
10. Regular Updates: Keep software and security tools up to date to protect against new threats.

Ultimately, a combination of education, technology, and responsible internet use can create a safer online environment for learners in classrooms. Trusting educational sites involves verifying their credibility, ensuring they are age-appropriate, and using sites recommended by educational organizations or institutions.

> Internet Safety—How does one teach *personal* social and cultural etiquette to promote safe learning environments for learners/educators?
> Authenticity—How does one develop protocols around truth and misinformation?
> Trust—What strategies check social media tools that are apt to be trustworthy?

INTERNET SAFETY

Etiquette is the code for polite behaviors. The Golden Rule applies here. Treat others as one wishes to be treated. There is a reciprocity among educators and learners, at the very least to be respectful and polite. How do we create environments of internet safety? Social means we do not live in a world by ourselves. The self must be juxtaposed between the self and others and belong. How do we develop a community that allows for growth, positivity, and safety through technology?

Question-Asking Strategies for Social and Cultural Etiquette

1. Increase wait time after questions have been asked. Give learners time to think of possible answers and examine how they came up with that idea.
2. Reverse roles: What questions would you ask about a learning episode if you were the educator?
3. Class motto: No question is a dumb question. Learners need to feel "safe" when asking or discussing learnings and reflections of what has been taught.
4. Celebrate the unique ways learners have different ways to get to the same queries.
5. Offer mirror stories (those tales that reflect the learners) to be listened to or read for discussion on ways the characters were treated and how they belonged.

How do we develop an armored self, own ourselves, and figure out our uniqueness? Are our selves only our experiences including others we meet and their shared experiences? How do we own ourselves? How do we learn about or adapt ourselves? Michael Jackson wrote a popular song about "The Man in the Mirror."[1] His lyrics, "I'm gonna make a change," suggest that in order to make a personal change, we must start with ourselves. Are educators "intentionally" and "deliberately" fostering personal growth, personal uniqueness, and personal/individual choice? The way others "see" us is a reflection, but is it a true reflection or a distorted one? What experiences are educators developing that help students reveal the person/learner who makes decisions, makes choices, collaborates, communicates, cooperates through technology safely? Tamping down on internet bullying is a strong goal. Some social media stories can be used for discussion that illustrate the consequences of certain behaviors.

AUTHENTICITY

Let's face it, social media posts are headlines that offer *simple answers or solutions* to very complex stories. It is striking how propaganda and disinformation can possibly persuade good people to commit to do bad things. How are educators/learners understanding the roots of their thoughts and their own behaviors? For example, which car insurance company gives you the truth about its benefits among these competing insurance policies: Progressive, Allstate, Colonial Penn, State Farm, Geico, or . . . ? The authors suggest that educators and learners do not surrender their free will and brains to artificial intelligence.

> **THINK/DISCUSSION BREAK IIIA: IS "TRUTH" THE END OF INQUIRY?**
>
> How can students be given opportunities to look for the facts beyond the headlines? What can be learned from television, radio, Facebook, YouTube, TikTok, Instagram, X microblogging (formerly known as Twitter), and Phone app commercials that go beyond the "product" headline? What ideas help educators and learners to manage artificial intelligence?

Technology and education can improve and facilitate learning. How do educators and learners transmit, gather, analyze, present, synthesize, hypothesize information that is explicitly or implicitly taught? Looking for patterns is a key to understanding what is presented. Technology allows for differentiation, collaboration, and cooperation as one becomes a truth pattern hunter.

Most students have a cell phone, iPad, Chromebook, computer, access to artificial intelligence, virtual reality, and so forth. People are still in control of the information on those devices. How are educators/learners seeking the truth? It is very apparent that some communities simply do not have access (economically identifiable neighborhoods and many rural areas where the internet is not available). What is the impact of the digital divide (those who have access and those who do not) have on teaching and learning? Almost everyone has a television—what programs promote honesty in contrived environments?

What is authentic? Is it a certainty? Verified fact? Constant? Conformity? Fidelity? Exact? Real? Assured anticipation? What is artificial intelligence? Generally, our technology is programmed by who and what information is put in. *Free choice is not about one's conditions but by one's decisions.* Technology must not take the place of critical thinking. Technology adds to our ability to make informed decisions.

> **THINK/DISCUSSION BREAK IIIB**
>
> Can one ever expect authenticity from technology? Are there any authentic posts that may be self-evident for educators/learners?

Teaching and learning must include ways to respect different points of view that build important relationships that allow for openness to curiosity and adventure. Technology—through its games, excursions, and simulated experiences—can be incorporated to extend the "life" of any learning episode. We are in a real reality but can use *virtual reality* to possibly teach the consequences of hypotheses of what could happen. The notion of developing hypotheses with possible consequences is a legitimate exercise in inquiry and developing curiosity and inquiry. How can educators lead learners to think outside the "box"?

ARTIFICIAL INTELLIGENCE—THE ELEPHANT IN THE ROOM

Artificial intelligence is data driven—it collects lots of information and therefore creates more risks. However, it changes schooling. There is *virtual reality*—requires a headset so one could be transported to an Italian village in 1861 or prepare for a rocket launch to the moon. One can look around the space and learn from simulations or still pictures. Then there is *extended reality*—requires a headset so one could now lift a basket and see what's inside the basket in the Italian village, or visit the inside of one of the homes that existed then. One can also examine the food packets that have been stowed and prepared for the moon journey. And then here is *mixed reality* that is a combination of virtual reality and extended reality but allows the user to interact with the scene and be trained on the intricacies of the technology to be learned or used. The user of extended reality can move the windows or the door in planning for a new house. AI supports Dewey's "learn by doing."

Students and most educators are familiar with AI as they video game and purchase items (like ordering groceries and clothing) for personal use. There are now prototypes call haptics that simulate the feeling of something "outside" reality. With haptics, one can feel the skin of a snake or fish. Imagine one is on a trip to a remote hiking spot and someone on the trip gets hurt. Perhaps a doctor or an emergency technician who is using the haptic technology can help the fellow hiker to save a life or administer temporary first aid measures until one can get more expert medical help.

Let's take AI into the classroom or at home or in a log cabin in the woods—Wow! By using virtual reality, extended reality, mixed reality, and soon haptic reality, solving large earthly reality issues is possible, perhaps even among challenged environments.

Right now, AI has already stored well thought out lesson plans with videos and artifacts to support learning episodes. The next iteration of educational books must feature what is available in AI and how best to use it.

THINK/DISCUSSION BREAK IIIC

What will sitting around in front of an AI device all day do to our physical and cognitive health?

NOTE

1. Michael Jackson, "Man in the Mirror," 1988.

4

✢

Motivating Learning by Throwing a Party

> A little knowledge that acts is worth infinitely more than much knowledge that is idle.
>
> —Kahlil Gibran

Objectives:

a. How does one build an on-ramp to include the community in fortifying instruction?
b. How does the educator get the community to contribute and provide feedback on learning objectives?
c. How may listening to shared stories increase learner engagement?
d. How can others help the educator and the learner extend the life of instruction?
e. How can the community help the educator/learner manage diversity, inclusion, and equity?

"Help! I need somebody."[1] How can educators collaborate, communicate, and coordinate instructional practice with and to "others"? Others, also known as investors—parents, family members, teachers, community members, and administrators—are all committed to how well educators affect the learners. Looking at some late night TV segments or Tik Tok footage when interviewers ask the "man" on the street to Name two countries in Africa; How many states are there in the United States?; or What is collateral when taking out a loan?, one wonders if what is learned in school is usable after school. Perhaps the questions asked by the interviewer are indicative of the narrow scope of what one thinks school should do.

The ideas for this chapter include collaboration, team building, and establishing relationships and accountability buddies.

The term *social soup* is used to talk about relationships that are robust, have lots of ingredients and are delicious as a whole. The soup metaphor suggests that relationships among learners, educators, and others enrich the learning experience. Learners and educators interact with a myriad of people. How can this social soup motivate learners to learn the instructional goals (either specifically or generally)? For example, if a lesson involves recognizing plant and animal cells, a biologist as a guest speaker could bring slides of those cells and ask learners if they see the commonalities and differences in the cell structures. Generally, the learning episode should gear the learners to reflect, describe, and/or hypothesize on the ideas that emerge. To extend the vibrancy of any learning episode is to ask others to participate. Student interviews by asking others how they think about, solve problems, manage variables, or look for answers reinforce for learners to know that they are not alone as they meet instructional challenges and/or successes.

HOW DOES ONE BUILD AN ON-RAMP TO INCLUDE THE COMMUNITY IN FORTIFYING INSTRUCTION?

Strategy I: Send home (or make a PSA [public service announcement] on school website) a biweekly syllabi of learning standards (what learners are to be able to know and do) to be covered with suggestions. For example, television and radio commercials, as they relentlessly repeat their product, can be used as a novel way to model learning standards. The educator is the seller so the "commercial" must come from them with help from their learners. Send home a YouTube video made by learners and educator that is catchy, kitschy, and clever about what the instructional goals are and ask for specific help. Provide the community (parents/guardians, board members, principals, community clubs) with emails or PowerPoints of what is expected of learners with available resources.

Strategy II: Community participation may include a monthly community conversation or a biweekly (bimonthly) virtual meeting at a designated time to discuss issues, a community academic night, table game competitions, a community theater production, a fun fair, a community tutoring picnic, a cleanup/repair task, or some other event that brings people together. Let's bring monthly assemblies back! Parents love to see their children perform.

Strategy III: A class website of learning goals coinciding with approximate teaching dates should be available with resources for enrichment or remediation. Have the community "sign up" as chaperones, tutors, crossing guards, co-teachers, instructional aides, lunchroom monitors, garden gurus, yoga instructors, and so forth as a way to include community. Those who sign up must of course be vetted to assure safety, privacy, and conscientiousness. Community recognition awards, luncheons, assemblies should be part of this collaborative strategy.

Strategy IV: Make a podcast or video and upload it on YouTube. Including the community is tricky but doable. It is interesting to see an attorney try a case—they talk with their client one-on-one, they get to research precedents, interact with the judge, the bailiff, and so on. A physician has that same bevy of people as they work with a patient one-on-one, a nurse is nearby and a receptionist ushers one in. With these professions, questions are asked, robust relationships have time to develop, a community/people are there to help. The educator, quite often, is alone. They have a myriad of variables to consider and receive nowhere near the salaries and yet they have so much more responsibility that has long-lasting effects. Educators need community participation.

Stories from Educators (Heros and Sheros)

Betty R: I had a super bright young man in my class with spastic cerebral palsy. It took him time to say his answers, walk from one classroom to another, and he presented, at times, involuntary movements. He had a one-on-one instructional aide to support his writing. He was eager and engaged. One day the instructional aide was not available. His classmates stepped up. Brian had taught his classmates about his differently abled condition and answered their questions. It was a marvel to see how he influenced their overall engagement in each lesson. I wonder why, to be frank with you; I am not sure what his secret sauce was but our class made tremendous academic progress.

Ruby K: It is not my style to ask for help and I did not know or live in the learning community. When the principal, who I knew from elementary school, asked that I help to arrange a book fair and a science fair, I thought I would crumble. I was moaning about it to my own mother and she said that she would help by making snacks for the participants. I went to the parent-teachers meeting and asked for time to ask for help. Wow, it blew my mind; parents and community members were signing up for providing prizes, food, photographs, supplies, and more. As my religious upbringing always said: Ask and you shall receive.

HOW DOES THE EDUCATOR GET THE COMMUNITY TO CONTRIBUTE AND PROVIDE FEEDBACK ON LEARNING OBJECTIVES?

Community tutors can be a vital support to the educator. Many times, the educator must tutor the tutor to ensure understanding of the content or skills. The educator can provide resources and conversation to provide tutor confidence and certainty. For example, a learner continues to have trouble decoding words that are multisyllabic. Tutoring a learner about the general rules of syllabication is very beneficial for decoding familiar/ unfamiliar words for any reading event *and* could be done by a retired educator in the community or a parent/grandparent or peer mentor. The educator must be intentional about asking the community for help. Before the learning episode (perhaps a complicated or challenging goal/objective), the educator can hold community conversations to include some of the generated opinions, ideas, methods around the goal/objective. Also, the educator could provide opportunities for some community members to "grade" or critique tasks around a learning goal. If the learners were given coded numbers to protect their anonymity, then the community could participate in more sensitive experiences. The community is vital for English language learners. Translators are always needed.

A Story from a Student

Ceci: When I arrived in Chicago from Paraguay, I expected to see friendly faces and welcoming hands. I felt ignored and like an alien. I was in a neighborhood where no one spoke my language, Guarani. Guarani is like Spanish, but not quite. I came from a rural area where our neighbors spoke only Guarani. I did not understand most of what was being said by both teachers and students. I cannot tell you how happy I was to meet a lady, walking her dog, who could help me with my Spanish and my English learning. My school actually permitted her to come to some of the classes to translate the ideas being taught. She was also instrumental in helping our family find two other families from Paraguay who also spoke Spanish and Guarani. I am in the University of Chicago majoring in chemistry. I travel back and forth to visit my older relatives, some of whom live in the big city of Asuncion, Paraguay, and they stress how important it is to learn Spanish, too.

* * *

The attorney gets feedback from his decisions from a jury pool; the physician gets feedback from the patient's well-being. The educator could use some help as they make curricular decisions and plan goals and objectives. The attorney, generally, specializes around some topic or theme (injuries from car accidents, nursing home abuse, criminal liability). The physician may consult with a collegial team around a problem to be managed or solved. The educator needs support for the community to step up and share their expertise where needed.

HOW MAY LISTENING TO SHARED STORIES INCREASE LEARNER ENGAGEMENT?

Strategy I: Sharing is a two-way street. Storytelling is an art form that has a myriad of benefits. If a learner is learning about the essentials for a school assembly around Black History Month, the educator may ask learners to interview or look online for family and neighbors sharing their experiences around the "story." Those shared stories can be archived like they do in the Library of Congress toward developing an assembly performance that could include video clips, songs, poems, and/or plays. Those shared stories will have commonalities and differences. The educator can parlay the gathered information to paint a picture of the tensions in the stories toward meeting an instructional goal.

Strategy II: Stories (appropriate) on tape gathered from the library or commercial vendors who archive stories are a great tool for quieting a room, giving a boost as a companion to a book of the same title, and great for attendance (can't wait to hear what happens in the next part of the story tomorrow).

Strategy III: Dissecting task directions so learners know how to approach and complete tasks assigned. Active listening (with visuals) is listening to the intent of the speaker. Active listening is intentional—paying attention to verbal and nonverbal cues; listening past the words to derive meaning. This is an essential learning skill for life. The speaker should not be interrupted. The active listener could be asked to summarize, paraphrase, and repeat what they heard. Encourage learners to be empathetic and ask questions for clarification; asking and answering open-ended questions and offering their opinion are all benefits of listening to shared stories.

The art of listening has been influenced by the visual media like television. The television does not listen or offer feedback. It just keeps on yakking. One can applaud, curse at, shed a tear, or be captivated by a television performance. The television does not care or respond. People's lives are interesting. How do we get those stories out without the makeup and lighting so that our learners understand how others celebrate and live? Television is not all bad; but you do hear actors and performers on live-stage say that their performance energy comes from their audiences.

Whether heckled or applauded, the performer (learner/educator) reacts. Are educators performers?

> ### THINK/DISCUSSION BREAK IVA
>
> What does communication conversation mean to you and how can you use it to enhance learning and instruction?

HOW CAN OTHERS HELP THE EDUCATOR AND THE LEARNER EXTEND THE LIFE OF THE INSTRUCTION?

Applying what has been learned is vital to extending the learning episode or concept. The community can help by co-creating hands-on experiences for learners to apply what they have learned. After a student lesson on measurements, a community project could be designing a school garden, or a small birdhouse or dollhouse. Students could learn about building tools—create a picture scrapbook of tools with their uses and prices; participate in building and funding a robotics lab. Cooking is a gateway experience to extend the life of academic subjects like world history, math, science, and social studies.

Getting community involvement helps learners keep up the school garden or care of the house plants. Community conversations around goals/objectives are key to ensuring that the knowledge and skills learned are *applied* in context. Learned knowledge and skills can be turned into internships, assistance, or applied science research. As of now, the educator barely has time to use the bathroom—getting help from the community makes sense and it can be orchestrated to get the best bang for the buck.

HOW CAN THE COMMUNITY HELP THE EDUCATOR/LEARNER MANAGE DIVERSITY, INCLUSION, AND EQUITY?

Celebrating learning differences is an essential tool to meet the need to belong. Celebrating differences in how living things function teaches respect and empathy. Being included and being inclusive is a valuable goal to learn. How does this happen? Field trips, field trips, field trips. Learners must get out and video record or auditorily record, or make art renderings of what they see and imagine. Equity or fairness is accommodated with patience and respect for others. Learning empathy and listening to others' stories may reduce violence, particularly when one uses words and not fists or firearms. The community must participate in understanding diversity, inclusion, and equity by creating cultural conventions where families can share their stories and sample food, music, dance, and art.

Strategy I: Bridging reciprocal learning relationships through cultural lenses. The concept of trust and its elements, as mentioned by Stephen Covey,[2] play a crucial role in the relationship between educators and learners. Building trust through competency, consistency, compassion, and integrity can foster a positive learning environment. Additionally, recognizing and respecting culture cues and fostering a classroom culture that values diversity and inclusivity can enhance the effectiveness of learning experiences. Educators need to be both humble and vulnerable as they manage any learning experience. Learners "see" the match between the educator's words and the educator's behaviors. Look, listen, wait, and allow learners to feel safe as they learn. Provide opportunities for learners to manage their thoughts as they make connections of complex information. There is a strong connection between culture and motivation.

THINK/DISCUSSION BREAK IVB

What might reciprocal learning relationships (learners and educators) through cultural lenses look like?

Gloria Ladson-Billings[3] asserts that the cultural forces that affect a culturally responsive educator provides learners with opportunity, time, models, language, environment, interactions, routines, and expectations. Educators must check their own biases. Educators must honor, explore, and extend the resources of the learner and their community. Meet the parents, guardians, shopkeepers, and visit the community institutions. Know where learners play, attend religious institutions, shop, what they get for birthdays, or how they participate in family traditional observances. Ask learners where they go to be alone and what they do to celebrate life.

NOTES

1. The Beatles, "Help!," 1965.
2. S. M. R. Covey, and R. R. Merill, 2006, *The Speed of Trust: The One Thing That Changes Everything*. New York, Simon & Schuster.
3. G. Ladson-Billings, "Culturally Relevant Pedagogy 2.0: A.k.a. the Remix," *Harvard Educational Review* 84 (2014): 74–84. https://doi.org/10.17763/haer.84.1.p2rj131485484751.

5

New/Old Instructional Strategies to Use

There is nothing new under the sun. Here is a compilation of what famous educator architects use to improve instruction.

INSTRUCTIONAL TECHNIQUES (JANET LERNER,[1] MARZANO,[2] DANIELSON,[3] AND GARDNER[4]—PEDAGOGY)

a. Representing the same content and skills in at least four ways: VAKT (visually, auditorily, kinesthetically, and tactilely)
b. Using the senses to connect content and skills socially and emotionally
c. Waking the students' and other investors' authentic, metacognitive, and multisensory connections to each other (Gardner, Marzano, and Danielson)

Instructional techniques refer to the methods and strategies that educators use to facilitate effective teaching and learning. These techniques encompass a wide range of approaches and practice in which the educator can aim at delivering educational content, engaging students, and promoting understanding. Here are some common instructional strategies:

1. Lectures: traditional lectures involve the instructor presenting information verbally to students. Effective lectures involve the storytelling, visual aids, and interactive elements to engage learners.

2. Active Learning: This approach encourages students to participate actively in the learning process. Techniques include group discussion, problem-solving exercises, debates, and hands-on activities.
3. Flipped Classroom: In a flipped classroom, students review course materials independently outside of class and use class time for discussions, collaborative projects, and hands-on activities.
4. Socratic Method: This method involves asking open-ended questions to stimulate critical thinking, encourage discussion, and deepen understanding of a topic.
5. Problem-Based Learning (PBL): Students work on real-world problems or case studies, which require them to apply their knowledge and critical thinking skills to find solutions.
6. Project-Based Learning: Students work on extended projects that require them to research, plan, and create a product or solution related to the course material.
7. Cooperative Learning: In cooperative learning students work in small groups to complete tasks or projects promoting collaboration and teamwork.
8. Peer Teaching: Students take turns teaching the material to their peers, reinforcing their own understanding and providing different perspectives.
9. Technology Integration: Using educational technology—such as multimedia presentations, online resources, and interactive simulations—to enhance learning and engagement.
10. Demonstrations and Experiments: For science and practical subjects, instructors often demonstrate concepts through experiments and hands-on activities.
11. Role-Playing and Simulation: Students act out scenarios or simulations related to subject matter, allowing them to explore different perspectives or hands-on activities.
12. Storytelling: Using narrative techniques to make complex concepts more relatable and memorable.
13. Think-Pair-Share: Students first think about a question or problem individually, then discuss it with a partner, and finally share their thoughts with the class.
14. Reflection and Journaling: Encouraging students to keep reflective journals or engage in regular self-assessment to monitor their progress and understanding.
15. Think-Alouds: Instructors verbalize their thought processes while solving a problem or analyzing a text, demonstrating critical thinking skills.
16. Gallery Walks: Students move around the classroom to view and discuss visual displays or exhibits related to the lesson.

17. Concept Mapping: Creating a visual representation (mind map or concept map) to organize and connect information, aiding comprehension and retention.
18. Debriefing: After an activity or project, instructors facilitate discussions to help students reflect on their experiences and extract key lessons or insights.
19. Feedback and Assessment: Providing constructive feedback on assignments and assessments to guide students' learning and improvement.
20. Culturally Responsive Teaching: Adapting instructional techniques to acknowledge and respect the diverse cultural backgrounds and experiences of students.

Effective educators often select and combine instructional techniques based on their teaching goals, the subject matter, and the needs of their students. Additionally, they regularly assess the effectiveness of these techniques and make adjustments as necessary to optimize the learning experience.

An educator can represent the same content and skills to learners in various ways to accommodate diverse learning styles, preferences, and needs. Here are some effective strategies:

1. Lecture and Presentation: Traditional lectures or presentations can be an effective way to convey information, especially for auditory learners. Use visual aids, storytelling, and engaging examples to make the content more relatable.
2. Hands-On Activities: For kinesthetic learners, provide hands-on activities and experiments that allow them to actively engage with the material. This can include labs, simulations, or interactive projects.
3. Visual Aids: Visual learners benefit from charts, diagrams, graphs, and videos. Create visually appealing materials that help illustrate complex concepts and relationships.
4. Reading and Writing: Some learners prefer reading and writing to absorb information. Offer reading assignments, textbooks, and writing exercises like essays, journals, or summaries.
5. Group Discussions: Facilitate group discussions or debates to encourage interpersonal interaction and collaborative learning. This can help students clarify their understanding and learn from their peers.
6. Technology Integration: Utilize technology and e-learning platforms to deliver content through multimedia formats, online quizzes, interactive modules, and video lectures. This caters to various learning preferences.

7. Real-World Applications: Connect the content to real-life scenarios and applications. This helps learners see the relevance of what they're learning and encourages deeper understanding.
8. Socratic Questioning: Encourage critical thinking and deeper understanding by asking open-ended questions that challenge students to analyze, evaluate, and synthesize information.
9. Gamification: Gamify the learning experience by using educational games, quizzes, and competitions. This approach can make learning more engaging and enjoyable.
10. Individualized Learning: Recognize that each learner is unique. Offer opportunities for self-paced learning, personalized projects, or alternative assessments to cater to individual needs.
11. Flipped Classroom: Flip the traditional classroom model by having students review content independently at home and use class time for discussions, activities, and clarifications.
12. Feedback and Assessment: Provide regular feedback on assignments, quizzes, and assessments to help students gauge their progress and make improvements.
13. Differentiation: Adapt your teaching methods to accommodate students with different learning abilities. Provide additional resources or challenges as needed.
14. Culturally Responsive Teaching: Be aware of the cultural backgrounds and experiences of your students and incorporate diverse perspectives into your teaching materials and discussions.
15. Reflective Practice: Continuously evaluate and adjust your teaching methods based on student feedback and learning outcomes. What works for one group of learners may not work for another.

A combination of strategies is the most effective approach as it caters to a broader range of learning styles and preferences. Additionally, getting to know your students individually and their preferred learning style can help tailor teaching methods to student learning styles.

Educators need to communicate to learners in different ways in the best way they can learn in four ways: visual, auditory, kinesthetic, and tactile. Visual learners need pictures and graphs to visualize, auditory leaners need to hear the information, and kinesthetic learners are those who need to engage in an activity in order to grasp a concept.

According to Richard Felder, "Approximately 65 percent of the population are visual learners."[5] Visual learners are often spatial learners and learn best through visual communication. This means using a whiteboard, projecting maps and images, or showing photos of your ideas work best. Visual learners have a great spatial sense, which makes them good with map reading and blessed with a strong sense of direction. They can easily visualize objects, so putting together a living room table from IKEA is simple for them when presented with a diagram of how the parts fit. Visual learners are often especially creative and get involved in design, photography, architecture, or professions that demand a good sense of orientation and planning. Visual learners need educators to communicate through maps, images, pictures, diagrams, and mind maps using colors and pictures in place of text, where possible.

"Around 30 percent of the population is made up of auditory learners, who learn best through hearing."[6] The best way to stimulate learning in an auditory learner is through discussion and group chat. Oral presentations and exams help this style of learner, or dictation and reciting what they have read or heard. Communicate by speaking for these learners. Try to vary your speech to keep it fluid and interesting. Auditory learners tend to like to discuss what they hear right away and ask questions. The use of songs and audio recordings is a great way for them to learn.

"Kinesthetic learners are a complex bunch and make up just 5 percent of the population."[7] These types of learners often struggle with learning through traditional means and sedentary activities like lectures and conferences. Their minds have a challenge in making the connection that they're doing something when listening or observing. They need to get up and get engaged in the action for it to sink into their memory.

One way to be truly successful in the classroom is to wrap your head around the four different learning styles according to Fleming and Mills's **VARK** (visual, aural, read/write, kinesthetic) model.[8] If you know how you learn best, you can use specific methods to retain what you learn in class. Different learning styles require varied methods to keep you motivated and successful in the classroom. Here is a bit more about each of the four learning styles.

Visual

Fleming states that visual learners have a preference for *seeing* the material in order to learn it.

1. **Strengths of the visual learner:**
    a. Instinctively follows directions
    b. Can easily visualize objects
    c. Has a great sense of balance and alignment
    d. Is an excellent organizer

2. **Best ways to learn:**
    a. Studying notes on overhead slides, whiteboards, Smart Boards, PowerPoint presentations, etc.
    b. Reading diagrams and handouts
    c. Following a distributed study guide

d. Reading from a textbook
   e. Studying alone

Aural

With this learning style, students have to hear information to truly absorb it.

1. **Strengths of the auditory learner:**
   a. Understanding subtle changes in tone in a person's voice
   b. Writing responses to lectures
   c. Oral exams
   d. Storytelling
   e. Solving difficult problems
   f. Working in groups

2. **Best ways to learn:**
   a. Participating vocally in class
   b. Making recordings of class notes and listening to them
   c. Reading assignments out loud
   d. Studying with a partner or group

Read/Write

With this learning style, students prefer to use lists, titles, notes, and headings

1. **Strengths of the read/write learner:**
   a. Studying using notes and headings
   b. Writing responses to class instruction
   c. Essay writing
   d. Solving difficult problems
   e. Working in groups

2. **Best ways to learn:**
   a. Studying lists, titles, notes, headings
   b. Bullet points, text-based formats
   c. Open-ended questions with a written response
   d. Studying with a partner or groups.

Kinesthetic

Kinesthetic learners tend to want to *move* while learning.

1. **Strengths of the kinesthetic learner:**
   a. Great hand-eye coordination
   b. Quick reception
   c. Excellent experimenters
   d. Good at sports, art, and drama
   e. High levels of energy

2. **Best ways to learn:**
   a. Conducting experiments
   b. Acting out a play
   c. Studying while standing or moving
   d. Doodling during lectures
   e. Studying while performing an athletic activity like bouncing a ball or shooting hoops

Generally, students tend to favor one learning style more than another, but most people are a mix of two or maybe even three different styles. So teachers, make sure you're creating a classroom that can engage any type of learner. And students, use your strengths so you can be the most successful student you can be.

NOTES

1. J. Lerner & B. Johns, *Learning Disabilities and Related Disabilities: Strategies for Success* (2014). Cengage Publishing.

2. R. Marzano & M. Toth, (2014). "Teaching for Rigor: A Call for a Critical Instructional Shift," https://MCO5-01-Teaching-for-Rigor-Paper-05-20-14-Digital-1.pdf.

3. C. Danielson, (2010). "Danielson's Framework for Teaching Classroom Observations," https://usprogram.gatesfoundation.org/-/media/dataimport/resources/pdf/2016/12/danielson-fft-10-29-101.pdf

4. H. Gardner, (1983). *Frames of Mind: The Theory of Multiple Intelligences.* New York, Basic Books.

5. R. Felder, 2002, updated preface to R. Felder and L. Silverman, "Learning and Teaching Styles in Engineering Education," *Engineering Education* 78, no. 7 (1988): 674–81, https://www.researchgate.net/publication/309120076_Learning_and_teaching_styles_in_engineering_education_Engr.

6. Felder, 2002.

7. Felder, 2002.

8. N. D. Fleming and C. Mills, 1992, "The VARK Modalitie: Visual, Aural, Read/write & Kinesthetic," https://vark-learn.com>introductiontovark>the-vark.

6

Instructional Consumerism
What Is It?

Instructional consumerism is a practice that educators use to narrow and focus their lesson goals/episodes and objectives. It makes learning episodes count, memorable and personally meaningful. The educator is the architect, and the learners are the consumers—who can co-construct their learning through questions and curiosity. Learners need opportunities to apply their "new" knowledge and skills in authentic (real-life, simulated) ways. How do we motivate the learners to motivate themselves?

Objectives:

a. Curiosities, Choice, Consequence
b. Independence
c. Self-Advocacy

CURIOSITIES

It is said that curiosity comes in four flavors: thinker, adventurer, observer, and solver.

THINKER: Aristotle says, "It's the mark of an educated mind to entertain a thought without accepting it." Exploring how multiplication can be used in English language arts and science, the curious learner may use a broader perspective and connect in ways that their classmates may not. How does the instruction to the thinker generate new ideas? Curiosity is a strong desire or interest that leads to inquiry.

ADVENTURER: Amelia Earhart's quote, "Adventure is worthwhile in itself," suggests an openness to ideas by drawing and attracting other people's ideas, culture, and thrill-seeking journeys. Who can one meet with, talk to, or find different experiences with other than their own?

OBSERVER: Leonardo da Vinci says, "All our knowledge has its origins in our perceptions." The learner and educator look for what's missing. What else is going on in this scenario?

SOLVER: Albert Einstein says, "We cannot solve our problems with the same thinking we used when we created them." Solvers have a penchant for breaking things down into smaller steps. This learner/educator will often play the devil's advocate. In solving a division problem, the instructor might ask, What other ways can one think of to arrive at the same answer?

Instructional consumerism means that the educator architect must develop lessons that appeal to these curiosity archetypes.

THINK/DISCUSSION VI

What educator strategies could hook all four curiosity archetypes for this goal?

CHOICE

Paraphrasing television talk show host Oprah Winfrey's gift of a new car to her 2010 audience: You get a choice; You get a choice; You get a choice. Both educator and learner should have choices. Homework assignments can be created to offer three choices of tasks. Learners should have opportunity to voice their choice by polling, surveying, and interviewing their classmates, educators, and any others that may contribute to their comprehension of a learning episode.

Strategy I: Co-constructing

The educator can *co-construct* instructional goals by modeling highly structured, sequenced steps. Then a skill can be taught by (1) preparing the lesson, (2) talking to students during the lesson to see if they understand it, and (3) blending learner and educator responses. The educator and learner work together to build the learning episode. For example, in a fiction/nonfiction assignment, one group of learners could show the elements of nonfiction and another group could do the same with fiction. Using explicit instruction while planning the lesson, modeling the practice and guiding the learner through a group activity gives the learner the skills to complete the task.

Strategy II: **Reshaping**

The educator can *reshape* instructional goals by reviewing data from quizzes and talking to students to find out why they didn't hit the target. Was it because they had trouble with the vocabulary or they didn't understand the assignment? Learners should be offered many resources to autocorrect or get help.

The instructional goal is like the bullseye on a target. The learner is the arrow, the objectives are the bow. The educator can throw "the arrows" at the target and hope they hit the bullseye, or the educator can restructure the bullseye: make it closer, push it farther away, or put it on the floor or a wall, whatever makes the target accessible for the learner. The educator may need to reduce the syntactic complexity, do call and response routines, reteach vocabulary, or create a rap song. Other options: using BrainPop (an educational website) or watching a YouTube video or a short movie to "reshape" the key elements of the learning episode.

Strategy III: **Reteaching**

An educator can *reteach* instructional goals in multiple ways of representing the same content and skills. For example, if the lesson is still on fiction and nonfiction, learners could complete starter notes (Post-it notes of questions that students need to answer as they read), comparing and contrasting, describing, listening to learning episodes while creating a class newspaper, a PowerPoint, YouTube video, Canva, and so on. Theater improvisation is a fun way to get across the lesson episode.

Educators can also allow learners to choose their assignments sometimes based on their learning styles. For example, if the assignment is to summarize a lesson on a book's setting, the learner could (1) draw a scene of the setting, (2) write a brief summary of how the setting is described in the passage, or (3) create a playlet for peers to perform using words to describe the setting.

Postscript

How does the learner learn the core disciplines? The educator can prompt the learner to connect core disciplinary tasks to something usable or applicable in a real-world context. A suggested learning goal (objective) could be: Can I recognize writing or verbal conventions like subjective clauses uttered in television commercials to persuade the public to use a certain product? Knowing grammatical rules, which are necessary for communication, is a must for after-school life. Students need to know how to write memos, letters, develop PowerPoints and Canva presentations.

A pilot learns to fly a plane, and safely navigate passengers to their destinations, by relying on their ability to read an instrument panel. Educators, like pilots, have a similar responsibility to their students, but they do not always have an instrument panel. Planning is the key to instructional consumerism and educator efficacy.

CONSEQUENCES

"The road to hell is paved with good intentions" (Abbot Bernard of Clairvaux, mid-1100s).

A teacher may have planned an excellent lesson episode, but the learners did not fully understand. Here are some planning strategies for imbedding core disciplines contextually.

Strategy I

Vocabulary instruction teaches words in context. Learners must be exposed to and use new words. However, putting up a word wall with no sentences (no context) looks nice, but it does not show learners how to use the words. What comes first, the learning goal or the vocabulary? Without rigorous, relevant, and relatable vocabulary teaching, the objective is difficult to understand and the "perfect" lesson plans are *lost* to the learners. Flocabulary or other vocabulary internet games are helpful. And learners must talk, talk, and talk some more.

Strategy II

Syntactic complexity is the challenge of understanding how an author is expressing ideas through complex sentences, which may contain multiple ideas or use unusual words. All of this makes it difficult for learners to comprehend what they are reading. But there are solutions like using a sentence scrambler that let learners manipulate and add words to sentences. A complex sentence can be broken down into two or three sentences. Learners could arrange words into a complete sentence using correct English grammar. This strategy may help learners develop syntactic awareness. The educator must recognize the syntactic complexity of a reading passage.

Strategy III

Literacy is phonological awareness, word recognition, and fluency. These skills are vital to more advanced or independent learning. Phonological awareness is the ability to orally identify and manipulate the sound units of language: words, syllables, and speech. Word recognition skills include analyzing multisyllabic words into morphemes (smallest units of meaning like prefixes [un-] and suffixes [-ing]). The learner must be able to decode (in many instances, familiar) multisyllabic words. For fluency, the learner must be able to connect text automatically with the proper pronunciation using volume and pace to convey meaning. Reading is fundamental. Literacy skills are necessary and cannot be ignored. Talk/speak about what was read and continue to talk/speak.

Strategy IV

Comprehension is understanding and interpreting what is read. The learners' inability to understand the written material, decode what is read, make connections between what is read and what they already know is challenging, and an inability to critically think about what is read are potential interrupters for meeting lesson goals and objectives. Every learning objective involves reading.

Here are a few ideas to embed the core disciplines of reading:

1. Conducting polls promotes student choice
2. Taking surveys promotes student voice
3. Interviews promote question asking
4. "Dear Abby" problems may boost social/emotional learning
5. Doing project-based learning in any discipline
6. Creating the rules for a robotic competition
7. Planning and planting school landscape
8. Analyzing social media platforms and creating new ones
9. Collecting old toys and remaking them into new ones
10. Reimagining drinking fresh water in the desert
11. Creating a photo documentary of classmates' lives
12. Creating and co-constructing a play, skit, or YouTube video of an assignment

INDEPENDENCE

"Remember, if you ever need a helping hand, you'll find one at the end of your arm."

—Audrey Hepburn

Independence, getting learners to be in charge of their own learning, is the educator's challenge. Students should do their own research and ask questions, rather than rely solely on materials provided by an educator. The learner takes ownership of their own educational path by setting their own goals with *feedback*.

SELF-ADVOCACY

Self-advocacy is the ability to "fight" for one's right to be heard, loved, and liked. It is confidence in one's ability to challenge and be challenged. It means communicating, negotiating, and asserting one's own interest and desires.

What strategies does the educator use to teach learners to advocate for their learning?

The educator can ask the learner to list their likes and dislikes and explain why they feel a certain way about specific learning activities. For example, a learner may dislike reading because they struggle to comprehend syntactically complex passages. If they are encouraged to self-advocate, they could ask to work with a peer to develop summarizing skills.

The educator could prompt learners to self-assess and reflect. "What are your strengths in this lesson?" "What do you often need help doing?" "What do you feel you learn best?" This self-reflection supports learners and helps them recognize where they will need to flex their self-advocacy muscles.

Educators can also

1. Encourage a bashful or unenthusiastic learner to safely make errors and ask for alternative options.
2. Use a digital poll to see a learner's response in real time and use the data to make changes in the lesson.
3. Provide learners with a question or a suggestion box where they can communicate their needs.
4. Help learners feel more confident about communicating their learning needs by using small group activities, partner work buddies, language frames, sentence starters, and call and response routines.

Educator Story

Mai Chen: I was teaching at an alternative high school for diverse learners who had intellectual challenges. I was teaching a science lesson about the components of batteries and how they work. I was able to get my cousin to cut a AA battery in half to show the three parts of the battery, which we named, explained, and drew and labeled a diagram. Showed the parts of a battery and mention[ed] that a chemical reaction made the battery work. We discussed what a chemical reaction was. I allowed for questions and then set up a lemon, a potato, and an apple sandwich. I asked students to predict which of the foods would have the most acid for a chemical reaction like the battery. Then we tested our predictions using an ammeter and then charted the results so everyone could see them. The potato won with oohs and aahs because no one predicted the potato would have the most acid. Finally, I laid out different shapes and kinds of batteries and different kinds of things that operated using batteries and I said, Make these work. The learning lesson was over time, but it was engaging and I was able to teach the words: *anode*, *cathode*, and *electrolyte*. Students were able to explain what chemical reaction means. Oh, yes, I was proud of myself and my students for learning some new words and to predict, chart, and know about chemical reaction.

* * *

What are some of the characteristics of self-advocacy?

1. Believing you deserve it
2. Shamelessly asking for what you want
3. Practicing positive self-talk
4. Tracking your accomplishments
5. Asking for help when you need it
6. Standing up for yourself
7. Being highly visible
8. Finding sponsors to help advocate for you
9. Showing up in situations where you can advocate for yourself
10. Becoming an expert in your field

Postscript

Researchers That Influence Educators for All Learner Characteristics

GARDNER'S MULTIPLE INTELLIGENCES

What are the learning profiles of learners through the lens of multiple intelligences? What kind of learner am I?

The theory of multiple intelligences is one way to have educator/learners identify their learning preferences. As Emiko said in the first story: She learned by researching answers posed by her teachers. Alana said she learned by reading it over and over before she understood. The authors have heard of people doing vigorous exercises while remembering different formulas. There are apps that have poetry and songs to help develop competencies and skills.

Learning how one learns is the genesis for Howard Gardner's multiple intelligences.[1] It suggests that learning through different portals helps the learner/educator grasp the deep understanding of a learning episode. Gardner introduced eight different types of intelligences: linguistic, logical/mathematical, spatial, bodily-kinesthetic, musical, interpersonal, intrapersonal, and naturalist.

GRIT: GUTS, RESILIENCE, INITIATIVE, AND TENACITY

Grit is a combination of passion for learning, perseverance at tasks, and purposeful activities. In addition, grit enhances student perseverance when confronting challenges, enhances academic performance, and help graduates stay the course in higher education.

There are four components to grit according to Angela Duckworth[2]:

1. Interest: enjoy what you're doing
2. Practice: conduct deliberate practice to improve on your weaknesses and continuously improve as you go, getting feedback from your experience as well as from others
3. Purpose: believe your work matters and improves the lives of others
4. Hope: believe in your capacity for achievement and ability to overcome difficulties

How does the educator "teach" grit? The educator can teach day-by-day experiences using instructional practices that model it. For example, a think aloud strategy, explicitly focused on teaching grit, is reading a complex text using the CLOZE reading strategy (uses passages of text with missing words to be filled in by using contextual hints); highlighting new vocabulary; and underlining main ideas and details. The think-alouds should also focus on how maneuvering a complex text is demanding and that making errors should be expected. A mindset of persistence is needed to be successful.

The educator can also teach grit by looking at how many strategies learners use to solve challenging problems. For example, the educator observes a learner solve a complex math word problem. How does the learner think about the information visually and concretely? How many strategies does the learner use to solve it?

In a reading lesson, the educator can teach learners to annotate text, take notes on the main idea, and search out difficult vocabulary words using a variety of tools and strategies so they can persevere through setbacks. Grit demands that there are many stages on the road to learning. The journey is appreciated and held in high esteem by the educator, which builds trust in learners. The educator needs to design time for the learner to change and assess the road to learning. *Feedback is key to developing grit. Learning to take constructive criticism also has to be learned* (especially in managing social emotional triggers).

The video "Austin's Butterfly"[3] gives an example on how learners can critique and give feedback and support grit in the classroom. The Grit Celebration Board can be a bulletin board or an electronic board where learners celebrate their own successes and the success of others by posting their accomplishments of perseverance.

MASLOW'S HIERARCHY OF NEEDS

How can an educator meet all levels of learners' needs with instructional practice toward self-actualization?

Maslow's[4] theory is presented in a pyramid-shaped hierarchy of needs. Basic needs (like food, water, and shelter) are at the bottom and higher-level intangible needs (esteem and self-actualization) are at the top. A person can only address the higher-level needs when their basic needs are adequately met.

The educator needs to be learner-centered to lead learners toward Maslow's notion of self-actualization. Every learner has different views, talents, values, and interests. The road to self-actualization may look different for each of them. Self-actualization is the fulfillment of your full potential as a person. Self-actualization needs include education, skill development—the refining of talents in areas like music, athletics, design, cooking, and gardening—caring for others, and broader goals like learning a new language, traveling to new places, and winning awards.

The educator wants learners to have the tools and resources to take responsibility for their own learning, to be their best and reach their full potential. The following activities can propel them toward that goal:

1. Use strategies and tools to get them to visualize their goals, write a plan to achieve them, and develop a strong sense of self awareness.
2. Connect them to resources and mentors that will help fulfill their individual needs and goals.
3. Help them develop time management schedules, checklists, and techniques for completing work.
4. Help them increase their skills in evaluation, self-assessment, problem-solving, and constant reflection, and if needed, reading comprehension, writing, and technology.

CALL TO ALL EDUCATORS

Now we invite you to go to Questknowlogy.org to add to the repertoire of questions asking strategies. Join the party! This party is to elevate and share the work of professional teachers. Our address is Questknowlogy@gmail.com.

The authors invite you to share your greatest instructional strategies and question-asking strategies. What does instructional consumerism mean to you? We will celebrate your professional expertise as you will be the co-authors of the next book.

NOTES

1. H. Gardner, *Frames of Mind: The Theory of Multiple Intelligences* (New York: Basic Books, 1983).
2. A. Duckworth, *Grit: The Power of Passion and Perseverance* (New York: Scribner, 2016).
3. "Austin's Butterfly," EL Education, 2012, https://www.youtube.com/watch?v=E_6PskE3zfQ.
4. A. Maslow, "A Theory of Human Motivation," *Psychological Review* 50, no. 4 (1943): 370–96, https://psycnet.apa.org/doi/10.1037/h0054346.

Index

Page numbers in italics refer to tables.

ability, learning, 3
academic vocabulary, 14
active learner, xiv
active listening, 43
activities, framework for, xiv
adventurers, curiosity archetypes as, 56
AI. *See* artificial intelligence
analysis, educator questions for, 23–25
anchor charts, 30
Anderson, Lorin, 25, 31n1
application, of problem solving, 27
archetypes, of curiosity, 55–56
architect, educator as, ix, x, 1, 6, 17, 55; instructions from, 47
archive, of information, 30
Aristotle, 55
artificial intelligence (AI), 36, 37–38
auditory learners, 51, 52
authentic, information as, 34, 36–37

Bandura, Albert, xii
basic needs, Maslow on, 65
basic questions, x–xi
Behaviorism, 8
Betty, R. (educator), 41
Bloom, Benjamin, 31n1; question asking strategies and tasks of, 25, 26, 29
blueprint, instructional, xii
bullseye, as instructional goal, 57
bullying, internet, 35

call, to educators, 65
challenges, for learners, xiii, 33–34, 40, 51, 58, 63; educators and, 3–4; intellectual, 60–61
characteristics, of self-advocacy, 61
CIA. *See* curriculum, instruction, and assessment
co-constructing, choice strategy, 56–57
Cognitivism, 8

Index

community, xiv, 3, 4, 34, 35, 39; DEI and, 44–45; fortifying instructions in, 40–41, 42–43
complex information, for educators and learners, 45
components, for learners, 17
concepts and skills foundation tool, for educators, *16*
confidence, of learners, 60
Connectivism, 8–9
consequences strategies, to motivate learners, 58–59
Constructivism, 8
consumerism instructional, 55, 56, 58, 65
core disciplines, 57–58, 59
cornerstone (quoin), of educator efficacy, 1, 2
Covey, Stephen, 45
critical thinking, 13, 31, 37
cultural and social etiquette strategies, 35
cultural lenses, relationships through, 45
curiosity archetypes, for learning, 55–56
curriculum, instruction, and assessment (CIA), 13

Danielson, C., 47–53
da Vinci, Leonardo, 56
DEI. *See* diversity, equity, and inclusion
designs, of teaching episodes, 1, 3
devices, technology, 36
Dewey, J., 37
differences, learning, 44–45
digital divide, 36
disciplines, core, 57–58, 59
diverse learners, 60–61
diversity, equity, and inclusion (DEI), 44–45
divide, digital, 36
division, of problem solving, 56
Duckworth, Angela, 64

Earhart, Amelia, 56
education, xiii, xiv, 1, 2–4, 14, 33; hierarchy of communication, x; learning objectives in, 29, 42, 59; purpose in, 1, 2–4, 33, 63, 64; technology and, 36–37; websites, 34
educators, ix, x, xi–xii, xiii, xiv, 1–4; call to, 65; challenges for, 61; community and, 43, 44–45; efficacy of, 23–25, 58; exit survey and, *18*; grit of, 63–64; instruction goals and, 56–57; investors and, 39; learners communicate with, 50, 51; learners relationships with, 40; lesson episode for, 17, 42, 55, 57; planning samples for, *10*, *12*; stories from, 41, 60; strategies for, 29–31; technology and, 33, 34; tools for, 8–9, *9*, 13–15, 17, 65; trust of, xiv, 2, 20, 36–37, 45, 64; truth seeking for, 36–37; unit/lesson samples for, 23–25, 27–28
efficacy, of educators, ix–x, xiv, 2, 13, 23–25, 58
Einstein, Albert, 56
engagement, of learners, ix, xii, xiii, xiv, 1, 2; increasing, 39, 43–44; learning styles and, 50–51, 53; school related, 4, 39, 41; technology, 33
English Language Arts, 14, 55, 58; learners of, 42; standards use around a POV in, *16*, 17
environment, learning, 33, 34, 38, 45
episodes, learning. *See* learning episodes
evaluation, of ideas or materials, 28
excitement, for learning, xii–xiii
executive functioning, xi–xii, 7
exit survey, 17, *18*, 18–21
extended reality, 37–38

feedback, 17, 39, 49, 50, 60, 64; community, 42–43
Felder, Richard, 50
five senses, as tools for learning, 17
Fleming, N. D., 51
fortifying instructions, in community, 40–41, 42–43
foundational knowledge, ix, x, 13–15, 31
framework activities, xiv
functioning, executive, xi–xii, 7

Index

Gardner, Howard, 47–53, 63
Gibran, Kahlil, 39
goals, xi, 15, 23, 24, 31, 35;
    instructional, 40, 43, 56–57
Golden Rule, 35
grit, of educators, 63
Grit Celebration Board, 64
group work, for learners, 31
guide, for learning episodes, 23–24

haptic technology, 37–38
hierarchy, of education
    communication, x
hierarchy of needs (Maslow), 65
high school algebra, learning standard
    sample for, *12*
how students learn, xi–xii, 15
Humanism, 8–9

ideas, for learners and educators, 1,
    13, 14, 25, 27, 28; learning episodes
    and, 36, 42; thinkers and, 55; visual
    learners and, 50
Illinois learning standard, 13
independence strategies, to motivate
    learners, 59–60
information, for educators and
    learners, xi–xi, 8, 15, 17, 24, 25;
    archive, 30; auditory learners and,
    51, 52; authenticity of, 34, 36–37;
    complex, 45; instructional goals
    and, 43; language of, 29
instruction, for educators and learners,
    ix–xv, 2, 8, 9, 15, 23; community
    involvement in, 39, 40–41, 44–45;
    consumerism, 55, 58, 65; goals for,
    40, 43, 56–57; grit practices for,
    64; lesson questions for, 24, 29;
    strategies for, 47–53
intellectual challenges, success story,
    60–61
intelligence, artificial, 36, 37–38
intelligences, multiple, 63
internet safety, 33, 34, 35
inventories, student interest, 15
investors, educators and, 39
involvement, community, 44–45

Jackson, Michael, 35, 38n1
juxtaposition, of self, 35

kinesthetic learners, 51, 52–53
knowledge, for educators and learners,
    ix, x, xiii, 8, 9, 13–15; community
    and, 39, 44; foundational, 31; ideas
    and, 25; instructional lesson, 24;
    observer and, 56; practices for, 30;
    skills and, 55; synthesis of, 28–29
Krathwohl, David, 25, 31n1
K—what do I know; W—what do I
    want to know; and L—what have I
    learned (KWL), 15

Ladson-Billings, Gloria, 45
language, and learning, xii, 2, 14, 29,
    42, 59
learners, ix, xii–xiii, xiv, 1–4, 7, 8–9;
    challenges for, 33–34, 40, 58, 63;
    community involvement and,
    44–45; diverse, 60–61; educators
    learn about, *18*; English language,
    42; foundation for, 13; kinesthetic,
    53; perseverance of, 64; skills for,
    14, 49; standard samples for, *12*;
    strategies for, 29–31, 55–61; styles
    of, 50–52; tools for, 15, 17, 65; trust
    of, xiv, 2, 20, 36–37, 45, 64; truth
    seeking for, 36–37; unit/lesson
    samples for, 23–25, 27–28
learning, ix, xi, xii, xiii, xiv, 1; ability
    for, 3; community and, 41;
    differences, 44–45; environment,
    33, 38; grit and, 64; language
    and, 2, 29, 42, 59; motivation
    of, 39, 40; multiple intelligences
    and, 63; opportunities for, 4, 31;
    optimization of, 49; project-based,
    48; self-advocacy for, 60–61; skills
    for, 43; social emotional and,
    33–35; standard sample high school
    algebra for, *12*; styles, 50–53, 56–57;
    technology and, 36, 37; tools for,
    8–9, *9*, 13–15, 17, 65
learning episodes, ix, x, xii–xiii, 8, *9*,
    15; community and, 44; educators

and, 17, 42, 55; educators learn how, *18*; guide for, 23–24; ideas and, 36, 42; learners and, 31, 40, 56, 58; multiple intelligences and, 63; teaching and, 1, 3, 47; technology and, 33, 37, 38, 57
Lerner, Janet, 47–53
lesson, for student learning, 60–61
lesson episodes, for educators, 17, 42, 55, 57, 58
lesson instruction, for educators and learners, 23, 24, 29
life, of instruction, 44
listening, active, 43

management, of misinformation, 34
Marzano, R., 47–53
Maslow, A, 65
materials, evaluating, 28
mathematical terms, 14
metacognitive, xi, xii, 7, 8, 15, 47; strategies for learning, 19, 24
Mills, C., 51
misinformation, management of, 34
mixed reality, 37, 38
motivation strategies, for learners, 39, 40, 55–61
multiple intelligences (Gardner), 63
multiplication, 13
multisyllabic words, 59

Naskar, Abhijit, 7, 21n1
new school, old school to, 4, 5
notebooks, as tools, 15, 30

objectives, learning, 29, 42, 59
observers, curiosity archetypes as, 56
old school, to new school, 4, 5
online environment, for learners, 34
opportunities, for learning, 4, 31
optimization, of learning experience, 49
organizational tool, for educators, 15
outcomes, for learners, 1–2, 8, 13
passive, learner, xiv
pedagogy, architecture and, 1
peer-assisted learning, 31

performance, television, 43–44
perseverance, of learners, 64
philosophical leanings, xiii
phonological awareness, 59
planner, for educators, xii, *9*
planning samples, for educators, *10, 12*
point of view (POV), for English Language Arts Learning Standards, *16*, 17
practices, knowledge, 30
prerequisites, basic, 13–15
presentation, of information, 17
pretest strategies, for educators, 14
problem solving, 3, 27, 28, 40, 48; division of, 56; strategies for, 64, 65
professional educators, teachers as, 7, 8, 65
project-based learning, 8, 48
purpose, in education, 1, 2–4, 33, 63, 64

questions. *See* specific topics
quoin (cornerstone), of educator efficacy, 1, 2

reading lesson, from educators, 64
read/write, as learning style, 51, 52
realities, xiv, 13; extended, 37; mixed, 38; virtual, 36
reciprocal learning, 45
reflection, educator questions for, 23–25
relationships, of learners and educators, ix, 27, 28, 33, 37, 45; social soup of, 40
research, learners and, 30–31
reshaping, choice strategy, 57
reteaching, choice strategy, 57
Ruby, K. (educator), 41

safety, internet, 33, 34, 35
sample questions, exit survey, 18–21
school, xii–xiii, 2, 3, 4, *5*, 7; AI in, 37; community at, 44; engagement, 39–40, 41, 43
screen time, students addicted to, xiii–xiv
SEL. *See* social and emotional learning

self, juxtaposition of, 35
self-actualization, 65
self-advocacy strategies, to motivate learners, 60–61
senses, as tools for learning, 17
shared stories, for learner engagement, 43–44
skills, for learners, 14, 15, 43, 49, 55, 59
skills and concepts foundation tool, for educators, *16*
Sleepless for Society (Naskar), 7, 21n1
social and cultural, etiquette strategies, 35
social and emotional learning (SEL), 33–35
social media, trust and, 34, 36
social soup, relationships as, 40
solvers, curiosity archetypes as, 56
spaces, for learning, ix
Spock (fictional character), 3, 6n2
standardized tests, 3
standards, learning, *9*, 13–15
standard samples, for learners, *12*
Star Trek (TV series), 3, 6n2
stories, 11, 16, 17, 35–36, 39, 41; of educators, 60; English Language Arts, 14; shared, 43–44; of students, 42
storytelling, 48
strategies, for educators, ix, x, xi–xii, xiv, 1, 2; community instruction, 40–41; instructional, 47–53; learner engagement, 43–44; metacognitive, 19, 24; to motivate learners, 55–61; question, 29–31, 65; social cultural etiquette, 35; for solving problems, 64
student interest inventories, 15
students, learning, x–xiv, xiii–xiv, 1, 2, 3–4, 42; lesson for, 60–61; sample questions for, 25, *26*; styles of, 17, 50–53, 56–57; technology and, 33, 36–37
styles, learning, 17, 50–53, 56–57
syntactic complexity, 57, 58, 60
synthesis, of knowledge, 28–29

teachers. *See* educators
teaching episodes, design of, 1, 3
techniques, instructional, 47–53
technology, for leaners and educators, xiii–xiv, 4, 33, 34, 36–38
television (TV), visual media as, 43
terms, mathematical, 14
tests, standardized, 3
theories, of learning, xiii, 8, 9
thinkers, curiosity archetypes as, 55
tools, for educators, 8–9, *9*, 13–15, 17, 65
treatment, of educators, 7
trust, of educators and learners, xiv, 2, 20, 36–37, 45, 64; social media and, 34, 36
tutors, community, 42

unit planning, 8, 23–25, 27–29

VARK, 51
virtual reality, 36, 37, 38
visual, aural, reading/writing, kinesthetic (VARK) model, 51
visual learners, 50–52
visual media, TV as, 43
vocabulary, academic, 14
Voltaire, 23

websites, educational, 34
Weingarten, Randi, 3
Winfrey, Oprah, 56

About the Authors

Bill Truesdale has presented, mentored, and trained principals in leadership efficacy strategies using critical thinking skills; consultant for school improvement.
   Dr. William Truesdale—billtruesdale2@gmail.com

Vinni Hall has presented workshops and professional development on teacher efficacy using question-asking strategies; consultant for school improvement.
   Dr. Vinni Hall—vinni547@aol.com

www.ingramcontent.com/pod-product-compliance
Lightning Source LLC
Chambersburg PA
CBHW021813220426
43662CB00006B/295